Called to Lead, Called to Serve

Called to Lead, Called to Serve

A 40-Day Devotional For Church Leaders

Called to Lead, Called to Serve: A 40-Day Devotional For Church Leaders
© 2025 Keith Clark-Hoyos

Scripture quotations are taken from the following translations:

- New Revised Standard Version Updated Edition (NRSVue), © 2021 National Council of the Churches of Christ in the United States of America. Used by permission. All rights reserved.
- Contemporary English Version (CEV), © 1991, 1992, 1995 by American Bible Society. Used by permission. All rights reserved.
- New International Version (NIV), © 1973, 1978, 1984, 2011 by Biblica, Inc.™ Used by permission. All rights reserved worldwide.
- Common English Bible (CEB), © 2011 Common English Bible. Used by permission. All rights reserved worldwide.
- The Living Bible (TLB), © 1971 by Tyndale House Foundation. Used by permission. All rights reserved.
- The Message (MSG), © 1993, 2002, 2018 by Eugene H. Peterson. Used by permission. All rights reserved.

Printed in the United States of America.

ISBN: 979-8-9987673-8-8

Published by Clark-Hoyos Publications
Topeka, KS

For more resources, visit:
www.ChurchTrainingCenter.com

To the countless volunteers who step forward in faith—pastors, treasurers, chairs, and officers— offering your time and gifts to serve Christ's church. Your quiet faithfulness sustains the body and reflects the love of God in every act of service.

And to Zulima, my partner in life and in calling, whose wisdom, steadfastness, and grace make this work possible.

Books by
Keith Clark-Hoyos

Called Together: A Spirit-Led Discernment Guide for Congregational Planning

Embracing Our Call: A Practical Guide for Church Governing Body Leaders

The Ministry of Money: A Treasurer's Role in the Mission of the Church

Serving the Call: A Training Manual for new Governance Body Members

Sacred Listening: Discovering God's Call for Your Life

The Heart of Stewardship, The Practice of Faith: Guiding Church Leaders in Spirit-Led Financial Ministry

Rooted in the Call: A Chairperson's Guide to Spirit-Led Leadership and Discernment

Called to Lead, Called to Serve: a 40-Day Devotional For Church Leaders

Introduction

Church leadership is a sacred calling. To serve as a pastor, treasurer, chair, or officer is to carry both the joy and the weight of guiding a community entrusted to God. Many step into these roles with love for the church and a deep desire to be faithful, yet quickly discover that the work can feel overwhelming. Meetings stretch long, responsibilities multiply, and the balance between spiritual life and practical duty grows difficult to maintain. In such moments, leaders may begin to wonder not only *how* to serve, but *why* they serve at all.

This devotional was written to help you pause, remember, and realign. Over the next forty days, you will be invited into a rhythm of Scripture, reflection, prayer, and practice. The goal is not to add one more task to an already full plate, but to provide a space of renewal—a daily reminder that leadership is first and foremost about walking with the Spirit.

The pattern guiding these reflections draws from four movements that shape faithful leadership: the grounding of *calling*, the sustaining gift of *energy*, the faithful use of *resources*, and the continual posture of *discernment*. These movements are not steps to be mastered but ways of life to be embraced. They flow together, teaching us that leadership is not about control or survival but about attentiveness, trust, and communion with God.

Each day's entry stands on its own, yet together they form a journey. As you read, you may encounter reminders of truths you already know, fresh insights for your current challenges, or whispers of encouragement for what lies ahead. Some reflections may speak directly to your personal role; others may draw your attention to the shared vocation of your congregation. All are written with one aim: to help you lead in ways that are rooted in God's call and sustained by God's Spirit.

You are not alone on this path. Leaders across traditions and communities share in the same struggles and hopes. More importantly, the Spirit who called you is the same Spirit who will guide, renew, and sustain you. May these days become a time of deep listening, of renewed strength, and of growing clarity as you respond again to God's invitation to lead and to serve.

1

Listening for God's Whisper

Leadership in the church is a holy trust. It is never simply a matter of keeping programs running, managing numbers, or ensuring an institution survives. At its heart, leadership is about walking faithfully with the Spirit in ways that invite both individuals and communities into deeper communion with God. Whether you serve as pastor, treasurer, chairperson, or officer, your role is more than a responsibility—it is a vocation. To lead is to take part in God's unfolding mission, to help a community hear and respond to the whispers of the Spirit.

Paul speaks with urgency and humility in his letter to the Ephesians: *"I therefore, the prisoner in the Lord, beg you to lead a life worthy of the calling to which you have been called"* (Ephesians 4:1, NRSVue). The starting point of all faithful leadership is this reality of calling. A calling is not just a task to be completed or a position to be filled. It is the deep truth that God has chosen to work through you and through the community you serve. It is both gift and summons. To recognize calling is to acknowledge that leadership rests not on human invention but on divine initiative.

This calling is always both personal and communal. For the individual leader, it brings assurance that one's presence in ministry is not accidental. You are here because God has entrusted something to you. This grounding allows you to endure seasons of weariness and doubt. It protects against the temptation to define leadership by personal achievement or external validation. For the congregation, calling clarifies identity. A church is not gathered merely for its own sake or for the preservation of tradition. It exists for mission, to embody Christ's love in a particular time and place. Leaders help communities remember and embrace this truth.

Ephesians 4 sets calling in the context of unity and maturity. Paul writes of the church as one body, urged to live with humility, patience, and love. Calling is never about elevating oneself above others; it is about strengthening the body for service. When leaders live into calling, they remind the church that vocation belongs to all. The work of treasurers, pastors, chairs, and officers is not isolated; it is woven together into the larger purpose of the community. To be worthy of the calling is to live in a way that draws others into the shared mission of God.

Calling, however, cannot sustain us on its own. Many enter leadership with clarity of purpose yet soon discover how demanding the work can be. Meetings extend late into the night, financial anxieties mount, and the weight of expectations grows heavy. What began as joy risks becoming burden. Here the prophet Isaiah offers a word of renewal: *"But those who trust the Lord will find new strength. They will be strong like eagles soaring upward on wings; they will walk and run without getting tired"* (Isaiah 40:31, CEV).

The context of this promise is crucial. Isaiah spoke to a people in exile, weary from waiting, questioning whether God had forgotten them. Into that despair, the prophet declared that God's power does not fail and God's strength does not falter. Those who place their trust in the Lord will be lifted, renewed, and sustained. This is not about human effort but divine provision. Leadership draws from the same source. Energy for ministry is not maintained by striving harder but by aligning our lives with the Spirit.

This does not mean leaders will never feel tired. It does mean that exhaustion need not define us. Renewal comes when we pause to rest in God's presence, when we remember that the church's life does not depend on us alone. Prayer, worship, silence, and community are not luxuries but necessities. They anchor leaders in the One whose strength never fails. Energy becomes not a matter of willpower but of trust. As we release the illusion that everything depends on us, we find ourselves carried on the wings of grace.

Energy is also tied to focus. When leaders spend themselves on activities that are disconnected from calling, weariness comes quickly. But when time and effort are invested in what truly matters, vitality grows. Alignment with calling transforms duty into joy, even when the work is demanding. Renewal is not the absence of labor; it is the discovery of purpose within it. Leaders who return continually to calling, grounding their energy in God's provision, are sustained for the long journey of ministry.

The conversation about leadership must also attend to resources. Churches cannot live on vision alone. They must attend to budgets, buildings, volunteer gifts, and time. Yet these resources are never ends in themselves. Jesus reminds us: *"Whoever can be trusted with very little can also be trusted with much, and whoever is dishonest with very little will also be dishonest with much"* (Luke 16:10, NIV). Stewardship is not about accumulation but about faithfulness.

The words of Jesus highlight trust as the central measure. Leaders are called to handle resources—whether abundant or scarce—in ways that reflect God's mission. A congregation's budget is not simply an accounting tool; it is a theological document, revealing what the community values. A calendar of programs is not just a list of events; it is a portrait of priorities. Every decision about resources is ultimately a decision about faithfulness.

This understanding reframes the anxiety many leaders feel about scarcity. It is easy to believe that limited funds, shrinking attendance, or aging buildings define the future. Yet Jesus teaches that what matters is not the size of resources but the integrity with which they are used. Faithfulness with little is the measure of readiness for more. Leaders who keep this truth before them guide their communities away from fear and toward trust.

Resources must always remain in service of calling. When resources become the starting point—when decisions are made solely on the basis of what is affordable or available—the church risks shrinking its mission to fit its means. This inversion confuses tools with purpose. The role of leadership is to align resources with calling, not the other way around. Budgets, buildings, and volunteer hours are gifts given for mission, not objects of preservation.

This does not mean resources are unimportant. They are vital, but their significance lies in their use for God's purposes. Leaders who hold this balance teach their congregations to see stewardship as worship, as an act of trust that God will provide what is needed for faithfulness.

Even with calling clarified, energy renewed, and resources faithfully stewarded, leadership requires something more: discernment. Discernment is the continual process of listening for the Spirit's voice, testing decisions, and remaining open to redirection. James offers this assurance: *"But anyone who needs wisdom should ask God, whose very nature is to give to everyone without a second thought, without keeping score. Wisdom will certainly be given to those who ask"* (James 1:5, CEB).

This verse situates discernment within the generosity of God. Leaders are not left to figure out everything on their own. When wisdom is sought sincerely, God promises to provide. The challenge is not whether wisdom is available but whether we are willing to pause and ask, to create space for listening, and to receive what God offers.

Discernment is never a one-time act. It unfolds as a rhythm, a spiral of listening, reflecting, testing, and returning again to listen. Rarely do leaders receive the full picture at once. More often, the Spirit illuminates one step at a time, calling us to faithfulness in the present moment. This iterative process requires humility, the admission that we do not see everything; patience, the willingness to wait when clarity has not yet come; and courage, the readiness to act when God whispers a direction.

Discernment also guards against a subtle but dangerous distortion in church life: the temptation to let resources dictate mission. Too many congregations measure faithfulness by balance sheets and attendance figures rather than by alignment with God's call. Decisions made only on the basis of what is practical risk losing sight of what is possible with God. Discernment reorients us. It asks first: *What is God calling us to do?* Only then does it ask: *How do our resources serve that call?*

The practice of discernment often feels slow. It is less efficient than rushing to decisions or following familiar patterns. It invites silence, prayer, and reflection before action. Yet in this slowing, leaders and communities learn to walk with God rather than run ahead on their own. The true goal of discernment is not simply the right decision but a deeper relationship with the Spirit. Each time we pause to ask, listen, and respond, we draw nearer to God.

Discernment is also marked by surrender. Leaders who practice discernment learn to hold plans loosely, open to God's redirection. They resist the illusion of control, acknowledging that the future of the church belongs not to them but to God. This posture does not lead to passivity but to responsiveness. It cultivates a readiness to change course when the Spirit whispers a new direction, even if it disrupts comfort or habit.

The fruit of discernment is renewal. Leaders freed from the burden of outcomes discover peace. Congregations that practice discernment together learn trust. Instead of clinging to resources or anxiously striving, they become communities attentive to the Spirit's voice. They discover that leadership is not about knowing everything but about walking faithfully, step by step, in communion with God.

The journey of leadership, then, is shaped by these movements. Calling roots us in God's purpose. Energy sustains us as we trust in God's strength. Resources are entrusted to us as tools to serve the mission. Discernment keeps us aligned, listening, and responsive to the Spirit. Each movement flows into the next, weaving together a way of leadership that is less about control and more about communion, less about survival and more about transformation.

This is the invitation of *Called to Lead, Called to Serve*. It is not simply to read reflections or complete exercises, but to enter a deeper walk with God through the practice of listening, trusting, stewarding, and discerning. The Spirit continues to whisper, "This is the way; walk in it." To hear and follow that whisper is the essence of faithful leadership. It is the path of renewal for individuals, for congregations, and for the whole church.

Day 1

"You didn't choose me, but I chose you and appointed you so that you could go and produce fruit and so that your fruit could last. As a result, whatever you ask the Father in my name, he will give you."

— John 15:16 (CEB)

Reflection

The words of Jesus to his disciples strike at the heart of Christian leadership: *"You didn't choose me, but I chose you."* These words remind us that leadership in the church is not primarily about human initiative. It is not about who raised their hand, who was available, or who seemed most qualified. At its core, leadership is a response to God's appointment.

To be chosen is both humbling and empowering. It humbles us because it reminds us that our service is not about us—it is about God's purposes at work through us. It empowers us because it assures us that we are not alone in this calling. The same Spirit who appointed us is the one who equips us to bear fruit that will last.

Every leader in the church knows the tension of doubt. Treasurers may wonder if their work with numbers really has spiritual meaning. Pastors may question whether their vision is strong enough to inspire. Chairs may feel the weight of holding a group together. Officers may serve faithfully but wonder if their contributions matter. Jesus' words speak directly into these moments of uncertainty: *"I chose you. I appointed you."* You are not here by accident. You are here because God has entrusted you with this role, in this season, for the sake of fruit that endures.

Leadership calling is never merely personal. It is always communal. The disciples were chosen together, and the fruit they were sent to bear was for the sake of others. In the same way, your calling is bound up with the calling of your congregation. Your gifts, your presence, and your leadership are part of a greater whole. When a treasurer interprets financial reports faithfully, it strengthens the mission of the entire body. When a chair fosters a prayerful and respectful meeting, the board can act in unity. When a pastor speaks hope into weariness, the congregation sees God's future more clearly. Each leader's call is a thread woven into the larger tapestry of the church's life.

Bearing fruit that lasts means more than short-term success or visible accomplishments. Fruit that lasts is measured in lives transformed by love, in trust built among members, in generosity cultivated within a community, and in faith that endures through seasons of change. As leaders, our task is not to force outcomes but to remain faithful to the One who called us. The fruit will come, not through striving alone, but through staying rooted in Christ.

This call also reorients our perspective. Leaders are often tempted to focus on control—on getting things done, solving every problem, or ensuring every detail is perfect. But Jesus reminds us that fruit is not manufactured; it is grown. Our responsibility is to stay attentive to God's guidance, to nurture the soil of community, and to trust that God will bring growth in due season.

To begin this journey of reflection on leadership is to begin with calling. Before we consider the energy leadership demands, the resources entrusted to us, or the discernment required in decision-making, we must first be clear on this: we are called. We are chosen. We are appointed. Our leadership begins not with what we do, but with who we are in God's hands.

As you step into today, hear again Christ's words: *"I chose you. I appointed you."* Let them sink in. Your role is not accidental. Your leadership is a sacred trust. And through you, God desires to bear fruit that will last.

Application

Take time today to reflect on your own leadership story. Write down one way you have sensed God's hand guiding you into your current role. Then, consider how your personal calling connects with the larger calling of your congregation. If you are with others, share your reflections and ask: *What fruit is God inviting us to bear together in this season?*

_____

_____

_____

_____

_____

_____

_____

Prayer

Gracious God, You have chosen and appointed us for this time and place. Quiet our doubts and fears, and remind us that we are not here by accident but by Your Spirit's design. Help us to trust Your call, to serve with humility, and to bear fruit that lasts. Unite our personal gifts with the shared calling of Your church, so that our leadership may reflect Your love and bring life to the world. Amen.

Day 2

"I knew you before you were formed within your mother's womb; before you were born I sanctified you and appointed you as my spokesman to the world."

— Jeremiah 1:5 (TLB)

Reflection

God's call to Jeremiah reveals something astonishing: before his first breath, before he could shape a word, God already knew him, sanctified him, and appointed him. These words echo across time, assuring us that our own leadership, too, begins not with accident or human choice, but with God's prior knowledge and purpose.

Jeremiah was young, hesitant, and unsure of himself. He questioned his adequacy. Many leaders in the church today share those doubts. The treasurer wonders if financial skills are truly spiritual gifts. The pastor wonders if their words will be enough to sustain a weary congregation. The chair feels the burden of guiding difficult conversations with grace. Officers may serve faithfully but wonder if their quiet acts of diligence matter. God's declaration to Jeremiah speaks directly into such doubts: *"I knew you. I sanctified you. I appointed you."*

The truth of calling reshapes how we understand leadership. It tells us that long before others nominated us, before a committee asked us, or before we volunteered, God had already placed within us the seeds of leadership. This prior knowledge means that our gifts, experiences, and even our struggles are not wasted. They are woven into God's preparation for the work entrusted to us now.

Communal discernment is rooted in this conviction. If God has known and appointed each leader, then the body of Christ is not an accident of circumstance but a deliberate gathering of gifts. The treasurer's precision, the chair's steadiness, the pastor's vision, and the officer's faithfulness come together as different notes in a shared song. Each calling matters, and together they form the harmony of the church's witness.

Spirit-led stewardship grows out of this same awareness. To steward leadership well is to treat it as a trust rather than a possession. Jeremiah's call reminds us that we do not belong to ourselves. We belong to the One who set us apart. Leadership is not about control but about surrender— listening for God's direction and guiding others in faithfulness. When we remember that God has already gone before us, we can lead with both humility and confidence.

There will be times when the road feels uncertain. Jeremiah's ministry was full of opposition and hardship. Yet his assurance came from knowing that

God's call preceded the challenges. The same is true for us. We may not know every step ahead, but we can trust that the One who knew us before we were born is also the One who equips us now.

Calling also invites us to see our leadership not as an individual journey but as part of God's larger mission. Jeremiah was appointed not for his own sake but to be a voice for God's people. Likewise, we are called not to build our own reputations but to nurture the life of the church and to embody God's love in the world. Our calling is always for the sake of others.

As leaders, we are invited to rest in this assurance: we are known, sanctified, and appointed. Our leadership is not random, nor is it fragile. It is rooted in God's eternal purpose. When doubts creep in, return to these words. When leadership feels heavy, remember: the God who knew you before you were born is the same God who walks with you now.

Application

Take time to write down one fear or doubt you carry about your leadership role. Then respond to it in writing with these words: *"But God knew me, sanctified me, and appointed me."* Reflect on how that truth might reframe your fear. If you are in a group, share your reflections with others and invite them to name how God's prior knowledge might bring new confidence to their own leadership.

Prayer

God who knows us fully, thank You for calling us long before we understood ourselves. Quiet our doubts with the assurance that You have sanctified and appointed us for this season. Help us to trust Your preparation and to serve with courage, humility, and love. Unite our gifts for the good of Your church, and guide us so that our leadership bears fruit that honors You. Amen.

Day 3

"But in fact God has placed the parts in the body, every one of them, just as he wanted them to be."

— 1 Corinthians 12:18 (NIV)

Reflection

Paul's image of the church as a body is one of the most powerful metaphors for leadership and calling. Every part is intentionally placed. Every role is purposeful. None are unnecessary. This means that your leadership—whether as pastor, treasurer, chair, or officer—is not an accident of circumstance or a matter of chance. It is the Spirit's design.

When we step into leadership, we may sometimes doubt whether we truly belong. We compare ourselves with others or feel overshadowed by gifts that appear more visible. But Paul reminds us that each part of the body is arranged "just as he wanted them to be." This assurance means that God not only knows who you are but has chosen you to serve in a way no one else can.

This is not only about individual placement but about the health of the whole. A treasurer's careful attention to resources builds trust and strengthens the mission. A chairperson's capacity to guide discussions with steadiness and grace allows space for the Spirit to move in decision-making. A pastor's vision and preaching can awaken a congregation to God's unfolding future. An officer's quiet service provides the faithful consistency that holds a community together. Each of these roles, distinct as they are, contributes to the flourishing of the body.

Communal discernment rests on this truth. Leadership is not about isolated effort but about honoring how each person's call contributes to the larger whole. The body suffers when any part is diminished or undervalued. Likewise, the church thrives when leaders recognize that their calling is bound up with others'. Our gifts may be different, but they are not in competition. They are complementary.

Spirit-led stewardship grows from the same conviction. To be placed in the body is to hold responsibility for the good of the whole. We do not lead for our own recognition or advancement. We lead as stewards of the community's trust and of God's mission. Stewardship means using our gifts faithfully, encouraging others in their gifts, and creating space for the Spirit to bind us together.

There is deep freedom in recognizing this. You are not asked to be everything. You are asked to be faithful in the place God has appointed you. When you focus on living fully into your role, you strengthen the body in ways no one else can. The pastor does not need to become the treasurer; the treasurer does not need to take on the pastor's vision. The chair does not need to preach; the officer does not need to chair. Each is called to serve in the place God has arranged, and together the body bears witness to Christ.

This truth also reshapes how we view differences. Too often in the church, diversity of gifts becomes a source of conflict rather than strength. Yet Paul insists that diversity is by design. The body requires both hands and feet, both eyes and ears. In the same way, the church requires visionary leaders and detail-oriented servants, public voices and quiet encouragers. Unity does not mean sameness. Unity means many roles working together toward one hope.

As you reflect on your leadership today, consider how God has placed you in your congregation "just as he wanted." You are not an interchangeable part. You are chosen, appointed, and necessary. And your calling only finds its fullest meaning when joined with others in the one body of Christ.

Application

Reflect on your leadership role. What unique contribution do you bring to your church's life—something that no one else can offer in quite the same way? Write it down as a statement of affirmation. Then, if you are with others, share your reflections and ask: *How do our different callings complement one another, and how can we honor each role as essential to the unity and health of our congregation?*

_____

_____

_____

_____

_____

_____

Prayer

God of wisdom and design, You have arranged the body of Christ with care and intention. Thank You for placing each of us in roles that matter, each with gifts that serve Your purpose. Teach us to honor one another, to celebrate the diversity of our callings, and to live in unity of Spirit. May our leadership together reflect the wholeness of Your body and the hope of our shared calling. Amen.

Day 4

"Your teacher will be right there, local and on the job, urging you on whenever you wander left or right: 'This is the right road. Walk down this road.'"

— Isaiah 30:21 (MSG)

Reflection

Leadership in the church often feels like navigating crossroads. Choices present themselves—how to allocate resources, how to respond to conflict, when to begin or end a ministry—and leaders wonder if they are taking the right path. In those moments, Isaiah's promise speaks directly into our uncertainty: God is not distant. The Teacher is "local and on the job," offering guidance when the road divides.

This image reminds us that calling is not static. It is not only about the moment we said yes to leadership, but about the daily posture of listening for God's direction. Just as Israel needed reassurance in its wandering, leaders today need the same assurance that the Spirit walks with us, whispering, "This is the way. Walk in it."

To be called means to be led. Leaders are not asked to rely only on their own wisdom or instincts. The call is to remain attentive, trusting that God's voice will clarify where our steps should fall. That voice may come through Scripture read with fresh eyes, through silence in prayer, or through the honest words of a fellow leader. Sometimes it comes as conviction in the heart, sometimes as peace that surpasses logic. However it comes, the promise is that it will come.

This truth shapes how we discern as communities. No single leader, however capable, hears fully on behalf of the whole. A pastor brings vision, a treasurer offers clarity about resources, a chair ensures focus and balance, and officers embody faithful service. Each role listens from a particular vantage point. Together, the voice of God becomes clearer. Discernment grows in circles of humility and attentiveness, where leaders slow down enough to hear beyond their own preferences.

Spirit-led stewardship flows from the same reliance. A treasurer who listens for God's direction does not see numbers only as constraints but as signs of mission and opportunity. A chair who pauses for God's guidance before speaking can transform conflict into dialogue. A pastor who trusts the Spirit's nudge may discover the right word to offer in a moment of doubt. Officers who remain attentive can embody care in ways that steady the congregation. When leaders listen, their work becomes less about control and more about trust.

Yet hearing God's voice is not always simple. There are distractions: the loudest voices in a meeting, the pressure of deadlines, the anxiety of financial strain. These can drown out the quiet whisper of the Teacher. That is why cultivating attentiveness is part of the leader's call. Attentiveness means stepping back from urgency, creating silence, and trusting that God's direction is steady even when ours feels scattered.

Calling is clarified not once for all time but again and again as we walk. The Teacher does not simply hand us a map; instead, God walks beside us, reminding us at each turn, "This is the way." This guidance is not only for grand decisions but also for the ordinary choices that shape the life of the church. Every act of stewardship, every word of encouragement, every pause for prayer becomes a way of walking in step with God's direction.

As you reflect today, remember this: you are not leading alone. The Teacher is with you, urging, guiding, and steadying your steps. Your calling is not only to take the road but to take it with confidence that God is already present on it.

Application

Take a few minutes of silence today before making a leadership decision, whether large or small. Pray Isaiah 30:21, asking God to speak into the choice before you: *"This is the right road. Walk in it."* Write down what surfaces in your heart. If you are with a group, invite each leader to share a recent moment when they sensed God's guidance, and consider how listening together might clarify your shared direction.

_____

_____

_____

_____

_____

_____

Prayer

Faithful Teacher, You walk beside us when the road feels uncertain. Quiet the distractions that keep us from hearing Your voice. Guide our steps with clarity and peace, so that we may walk in the way You prepare. Teach us to listen together, honoring the gifts of each leader, and trusting that Your Spirit is present in every decision. Keep us steady in Your path, bearing witness to Your love in all that we do. Amen.

Day 5

"In light of all this, here's what I want you to do. While I'm locked up here, a prisoner for the Master, I want you to get out there and walk—better yet, run!—on the road God called you to travel. I don't want any of you sitting around on your hands. I don't want anyone strolling off, down some path that goes nowhere."

— Ephesians 4:1 (MSG)

Reflection

Paul's words remind us that calling is not passive. To be chosen by God is to be set in motion—to walk, even to run, on the road God has placed before us. Leadership in the church is not about standing still or clinging to comfort. It is about responding to the Spirit's invitation to live into our calling with courage, humility, and perseverance.

This calling is both personal and communal. Personally, each leader is summoned to bring their gifts, experiences, and perspectives to the work. The treasurer is called to interpret financial life in ways that serve the church's mission. The chair is called to guide meetings with clarity and patience. The pastor is called to point toward God's unfolding vision. Officers and lay leaders are called to embody faithfulness through service that nurtures the body. Each individual call matters, but none stand alone.

Communally, the body of Christ moves forward together. A road traveled alone may grow weary or aimless, but when the church walks in step, discerning God's leading, the journey bears fruit. Discernment, then, is not simply about finding one's personal direction; it is about listening for how God is shaping the congregation as a whole. Leadership requires creating space where the Spirit's guidance can be heard in the voices of many, weaving those voices into a unified movement toward God's purpose.

This is why Paul's urgency matters. The temptation to sit still—to keep things as they are—can be strong in church leadership. Fear of conflict, fatigue, or lack of clarity can make us hesitate. Yet calling is not meant to be shelved. When leaders embrace their call, they set an example for the body. They model what it means to move forward in faith, not with reckless haste, but with steady, Spirit-led conviction.

Spirit-led stewardship flows from this same posture. Leaders are not asked to own the road or to map every detail of it. They are asked to steward the gifts entrusted to them and to encourage others to do the same. Stewardship means guiding with gentleness, correcting with humility, and using every opportunity to serve the church's shared mission. It also means knowing when to wait, when to act, and when to trust God to reveal the next step.

Paul insists that we not wander onto paths that lead nowhere. This is a reminder that leadership calling is not about chasing every opportunity or responding to every demand. It is about staying aligned with the road God has set before us. That road may not always be the easiest or most obvious, but it is the one that leads to fruit that lasts.

As leaders, our task is not only to find the road but to help others stay on it. We are companions and guides, pointing back to God's call when distractions arise. And when we falter or grow weary, we can be assured: God is still near, urging us forward, reminding us that we are called to walk with purpose and unity.

Application

Reflect on where you see yourself on the road of leadership. Are you moving forward with purpose, hesitating on the edges, or tempted to take a detour? Write down one way you feel called to "walk" more faithfully in your role. If you are in a group, invite each person to share how their role contributes to keeping the whole church on the road God has called it to travel.

_____

_____

_____

_____

_____

_____

_____

_____

_____

_____

Prayer

God of the journey, You have called us to walk with purpose, not to sit idle or wander aimlessly. Strengthen us to live into our calling with humility, courage, and joy. Teach us to listen for Your Spirit's guidance and to honor the gifts of others as we travel together. Keep us steady on the road You have set before us, so that our leadership may bear witness to Your love and grace. Amen.

Day 6

"Then I heard the Lord's voice saying, 'Whom should I send, and who will go for us?' I said, 'I'm here; send me.'"

— Isaiah 6:8 (CEB)

Reflection

Isaiah's encounter with God is one of the clearest pictures of what it means to be called. He experiences the holiness of God, becomes aware of his own inadequacy, and then hears the divine question: *"Whom should I send, and who will go for us?"* Isaiah responds with simple, courageous surrender: *"I'm here; send me."*

Church leadership often begins in much the same way. None of us feels fully prepared. Treasurers may wonder if numbers and spreadsheets can truly be part of spiritual leadership. Chairs may doubt whether they can guide discussions that carry so much weight. Pastors may question their endurance for the long road of vision and care. Officers and lay leaders may ask whether their quiet service matters. Yet the call comes: *Who will go for us?* Leadership begins when we offer ourselves—not because we are flawless, but because God calls us.

What makes Isaiah's response powerful is not confidence in his own strength but trust in God's purpose. The same is true for us. To step into leadership is to recognize that God's work in the world requires willing hearts more than perfect resumes. Saying "yes" opens the way for the Spirit to shape us, sustain us, and guide us for the tasks ahead.

This calling is never for ourselves alone. Isaiah's mission was for the people of Israel, just as our leadership today is for the sake of the church and the wider community. A personal response always unfolds into a communal purpose. Each leader's willingness—whether to interpret finances faithfully, to hold the group steady, to speak hope, or to serve behind the scenes—contributes to the church's ability to live into God's mission.

In communities of discernment, the question Isaiah heard is still alive: *Whom shall I send?* God continues to ask this of congregations and leaders. The response is not about one person carrying everything, but about many people together saying, "Here we are; send us." Leadership is strengthened when each role is recognized as part of God's sending, and when leaders learn to encourage one another in the call.

Spirit-led stewardship also grows out of this willingness. Leaders who answer God's call do not cling to control or insist on their own way. Instead, they steward their role as a sacred trust—listening carefully, leading gently, and serving faithfully. Like Isaiah, they understand that the initiative is God's. Our part is to respond, to be present, and to step forward when the moment arrives.

There will always be reasons to hesitate. Fear of failure, lack of clarity, or the weariness of past struggles can hold us back. Yet Isaiah's story reminds us that calling is not about what we lack; it is about God's presence and purpose. When we say, "Here I am," we step into a stream of grace that carries us beyond what we could accomplish on our own.

As you reflect today, hear God's question anew: *Whom shall I send, and who will go for us?* Imagine how your unique role—whether public or quiet, visionary or steady—might be part of God's answer in your congregation. Trust that your "yes" matters, and that through it God is weaving together a community ready to serve.

Application

Reflect on your own response to God's question: *Whom shall I send?* Write down what it looks like for you to say, "Here I am; send me" in your current role. If you are with a group, invite each person to share their response, and consider together how your collective willingness strengthens the church's mission.

_____

_____

_____

_____

_____

_____

_____

Prayer

Holy God, You continue to ask, "Whom shall I send?" Give us the courage to answer, "Here we are; send us." Quiet our fears and strengthen our resolve, that we may serve faithfully in the roles You have entrusted to us. Unite our individual callings into a shared witness of Your love, and guide us as we walk in the path You set before us. Amen.

Day 7

"I appeal to you therefore, brothers and sisters, on the basis of God's mercy, to present your bodies as a living sacrifice, holy and acceptable to God, which is your reasonable act of worship."

— Romans 12:1 (NRSVue)

Reflection

Paul's appeal to present our whole selves to God reminds us that calling is not a part-time invitation. Leadership in the church is not something we pick up only during meetings or Sunday worship. It is a way of life shaped by offering ourselves fully to God's purpose. To be a living sacrifice means that every decision, every word, and every act of leadership becomes an offering of worship.

For church leaders, this calling is deeply personal. It means allowing God to shape the way we lead from within, aligning our motives and our actions with Christ's example. A treasurer presents their diligence not merely as bookkeeping but as stewardship offered to God. A pastor presents their vision not for personal acclaim but as a sacrifice of service to the gospel. A chair offers their ability to guide dialogue not as control but as a gift of order and peace. Officers bring their faithful presence, often unseen, as a holy act of devotion. Each role becomes an altar where leadership is transformed into worship.

Yet this calling is also communal. Paul addresses not individuals in isolation but "brothers and sisters." Presenting ourselves as living sacrifices is a collective act. The church thrives when its leaders see their varied offerings not as competing sacrifices but as shared contributions to the same altar. When leaders embody humility, patience, and faithfulness together, they strengthen the unity of the body.

Communal discernment depends on this shared surrender. Leaders who approach decisions with open hands, willing to lay aside ego and personal preference, create space for the Spirit to guide. A group that seeks not to win arguments but to honor God with their collective offering will find clarity in surprising ways. This kind of discernment requires trust: trust in God, trust in one another, and trust that even our ordinary efforts can become holy when surrendered.

Spirit-led stewardship grows naturally from this posture. Leaders are entrusted not only with tasks but with people, stories, and hopes. To present ourselves as living sacrifices is to approach leadership with reverence for what has been entrusted to us. It is to see budgets as testimonies, meetings as opportunities for formation, and decisions as moments to reflect God's love. Stewardship in this sense is not about scarcity or control but about offering our best back to God.

There is a cost to this call. Sacrifice implies giving up something—our comfort, our certainty, our desire for recognition. But it also brings freedom. When leadership is lived as worship, we no longer measure success by human standards alone. We measure it by faithfulness, by the fruit of love and justice, by the peace and trust that grow in the body.

Paul frames this act of offering as "reasonable." It is not extraordinary for leaders to give themselves in this way; it is the natural response to God's mercy. We lead not out of obligation but out of gratitude. We serve not because the work is easy but because God has been faithful. And in that gratitude, leadership becomes more than a responsibility—it becomes a joyful response to the One who calls and equips us.

Application

Reflect on what it means for your leadership to be a "living sacrifice." What part of yourself—your time, your gifts, your preferences—might God be inviting you to place on the altar of service? Write down one step you can take this week to embody leadership as worship. If you are in a group, share your reflections and ask: *How can our leadership together become an offering to God?*

_____

_____

_____

_____

_____

_____

_____

_____

Prayer

Merciful God, You call us to present our whole selves as living sacrifices. Take our leadership, our gifts, and our daily work, and make them holy in Your sight. Free us from pride and fear, and teach us to serve with gratitude and joy. Unite us as one body, offering ourselves together as worship, so that our leadership may honor You and bear witness to Your love in the world. Amen.

Day 8

"Each of you should use whatever gift you have received to serve others, as faithful stewards of God's grace in its various forms."

— 1 Peter 4:10 (NIV)

Reflection

Peter's words remind us that every gift entrusted to us comes with a purpose: to serve others. Leadership in the church is not about status or authority, but about stewardship—faithfully tending the grace of God as it flows through us in unique and varied ways.

Every leader has been given something distinct. A treasurer's careful management of finances is not simply a practical necessity; it is a visible expression of God's grace through accountability and trust. A chair's ability to guide dialogue and hold space for differing voices becomes an act of grace that nurtures unity. A pastor's preaching and visioning are not performances but a means by which God's grace is proclaimed and embodied. Officers and lay leaders, often in quieter ways, carry grace through steadfast presence, encouragement, and service. Each role, each gift, each act of faithfulness reveals a facet of God's generosity.

Personal calling is experienced in the recognition of these gifts. Each of us has been entrusted with abilities, passions, and perspectives that are not accidents. They are woven into our being by God, not for self-advancement, but for the good of the community. When we recognize our gifts as grace rather than possession, our leadership shifts from control to offering. We see ourselves not as owners of talent but as stewards of God's abundance.

Communal calling emerges when these varied gifts are brought together. Peter emphasizes "various forms," reminding us that the grace of God is too rich to be expressed in only one way. The body of Christ requires many kinds of gifts working in harmony. When leaders honor one another's contributions, they reveal the fullness of God's grace to the community. When one gift overshadows the others, the body becomes lopsided. True leadership is not about elevating a single role but about weaving them all into a shared witness of grace.

This is why discernment in community matters so deeply. A treasurer alone cannot define the mission, nor can a pastor carry it alone. Chairs, officers, and all leaders must listen together, trusting that the Spirit is at work in the diversity of gifts. Discerning God's call for a congregation involves attending to how grace shows up in its many forms and aligning leadership so those gifts can flourish.

Spirit-led stewardship flows naturally from this understanding. To steward well is to use what we have been given with faithfulness, humility, and generosity. Leaders who see their work as stewardship resist the temptation to hoard credit or power. They recognize that their gifts are temporary trusts, meant to be poured out for the sake of others. This posture transforms even routine tasks into holy acts of service.

The call, then, is not simply to acknowledge our gifts but to put them to work. Peter insists that grace is meant to be used. A gift left idle is a missed opportunity for the body to experience God's abundance. Leaders are called to offer themselves fully, trusting that their contributions—however small they may seem—are essential to the life of the church.

As you reflect today, consider how your leadership is a channel of God's grace. Your calling is not only to serve faithfully in your role but to recognize and celebrate the ways others are serving too. Together, your varied offerings reveal the beauty and richness of God's love in the life of the community.

Application

Write down one gift you believe God has entrusted to you in your leadership role. Then write how that gift serves others in your congregation. If you are in a group, share your reflections and discuss: *What different gifts do we see among us, and how do they complement one another as expressions of God's grace?*

_____

_____

_____

_____

_____

_____

Prayer

Generous God, You have entrusted us with gifts that reflect Your grace in many forms. Teach us to steward these gifts with humility, faithfulness, and joy. Help us to see our leadership not as ownership but as service, offered for the good of others. Unite our varied callings into a witness of Your abundant love, so that the church may reflect Your generosity to the world. Amen.

Day 9

"By the skill of his hands he led them."

— Psalm 78:72 (TLB)

Reflection

Psalm 78 reflects on the leadership of David, describing a shepherd who guided God's people with both integrity of heart and skill of hand. This brief but profound verse reminds us that leadership is not only about inner conviction or outer action, but about the integration of both. God calls leaders to lead with faithfulness of spirit and with the gifts, abilities, and wisdom they have been given.

For church leaders, this balance is essential. Integrity of heart anchors leadership in humility and devotion. Without it, skill risks becoming manipulation or control. Skill of hand grounds leadership in competence and care. Without it, integrity risks becoming sentiment without substance. David's example suggests that the two must come together—devotion to God shaping the heart, and practiced gifts equipping the hands.

Every leader brings unique skills to their role. Treasurers exercise precision and stewardship, ensuring that financial practices are trustworthy and transparent. Chairs guide conversation, helping boards stay focused and united in mission. Pastors cast vision and proclaim God's word, equipping the community to live faithfully. Officers and lay leaders model dependability, embodying service that holds the community together. These skills are not secondary to calling; they are part of it.

At the same time, skills are never enough on their own. The heart matters. A treasurer without integrity risks reducing financial leadership to numbers rather than mission. A chair without humility may use their position to dominate rather than to serve. A pastor without love may preach with eloquence but lack compassion. Skills become faithful expressions of leadership only when shaped by hearts aligned with God's purposes.

Communal discernment grows out of this balance. Leaders who bring both integrity and skill invite others into trust. When boards see humility guiding decisions, they listen more deeply. When congregations see competence applied faithfully, they follow with confidence. Discernment is not about one voice dominating, but about leaders together stewarding both heart and hand for the sake of the community's direction.

Spirit-led stewardship grows from the same integration. Leaders are called to nurture their skills as gifts entrusted to them, not for self-advancement but for the good of the body. Sharpening those skills—whether in finance, teaching, administration, or pastoral care—is an act of stewardship when done in service of God's mission. At the same time, leaders are called to continually return their hearts to God, seeking humility, patience, and love to guide the use of those skills.

David's leadership was not perfect. He stumbled and failed, as all leaders do. Yet the psalm remembers him as one who brought together the heart and the hand in service to God's people. This is a hopeful reminder: our leadership does not need to be flawless to be faithful. What matters is the ongoing willingness to align our hearts with God's will and to use our skills as instruments of grace.

As you reflect today, consider both the heart and the hand in your leadership. Where is God inviting you to deepen integrity? Where is God calling you to sharpen your skills? And how might these together bear fruit for the life of your congregation?

Application

Take time to list two areas of your leadership—one of the heart (such as humility, patience, compassion) and one of the hand (such as administration, communication, financial stewardship). Reflect on how these two work together in your role. If you are in a group, share your reflections and ask: *How do integrity and skill together shape our shared calling as leaders?*

_____

_____

_____

_____

_____

_____

Prayer

God of shepherds and leaders, You call us to serve with both heart and hand. Shape our integrity so that our motives are rooted in love for You and Your people. Strengthen our skills so that we may serve with wisdom and care. Teach us to bring these together in faithful leadership, that our lives may reflect Your calling and guide Your church with humility and strength. Amen.

Day 10

"But don't act like them. If you want to be great, you must be the servant of all the others. And if you want to be first, you must be the slave of the rest. The Son of Man did not come to be a slave master, but a slave who will give his life to rescue many people."

— Matthew 20:26–28 (CEV)

Reflection

In this passage, Jesus turns the world's understanding of leadership upside down. Greatness is not found in power or control, but in service. True leadership, he says, is not about being above others but about kneeling alongside them. The very Son of God, who had every reason to demand honor, chose instead to embody servanthood—giving his life for the sake of others.

For church leaders, this redefines what it means to be called. Treasurers are not called merely to manage resources but to steward them as acts of service to God's people. Chairs are not called to control discussions but to create space where voices are heard and the Spirit can be discerned. Pastors are not called to command authority but to shepherd, guide, and equip the body. Officers and lay leaders are not called to fill roles quietly but to embody faithfulness that holds the community together. Each calling is an invitation into service, not status.

This calling is deeply countercultural. In most organizations, leadership is measured by visibility, recognition, and influence. But Jesus points us in another direction: leadership is measured by humility, sacrifice, and the willingness to serve even when it is costly. Greatness in the kingdom of God is revealed in acts of service that may never be noticed by the world.

Communal discernment grows from this posture of humility. When leaders approach decisions not with the goal of winning or controlling but with the desire to serve, the body is strengthened. Listening becomes deeper. Differences become opportunities for learning rather than sources of division. The Spirit's direction becomes clearer when leaders place service above self.

Spirit-led stewardship flows naturally from this vision. Leaders who see themselves as servants resist the temptation to treat their roles as possessions. Instead, they hold their leadership with open hands, asking: *How can I use what I have been entrusted with to serve the whole body?* This question reframes even difficult tasks. Financial reports, committee meetings, sermon preparation, or administrative duties become opportunities for service, acts of love offered to God and neighbor.

The model is Christ himself. Jesus did not come to "be served" but to serve, and his service was not half-hearted. It was total, even to the point of giving his life. Leaders who follow him are called to mirror that same depth of commitment. While few are asked to make such ultimate sacrifices, all are asked to embrace a willingness to put others first, to choose service over prestige, and to lead with love at the center.

This vision of leadership is not only personal but communal. When a board, a staff, or a congregation embraces servant leadership together, the church becomes a living witness of Christ's way. In a world hungry for power, such communities embody a different story—the story of love poured out in service.

As you reflect today, hear Jesus' words as both challenge and invitation. You have been called to lead, but your greatness will not be measured by position. It will be measured by how fully your leadership reflects the servant heart of Christ.

Application

Consider one area of your leadership where you might be tempted to seek recognition or control. Write down one concrete way you can instead embody servant leadership in that area this week. If you are with others, share your reflections and ask: *How can our leadership together reflect Christ's model of service more fully?*

_____

_____

_____

_____

_____

_____

_____

Prayer

Servant Lord, You showed us that true greatness is found in service. Shape our hearts to follow Your example. Free us from the desire for recognition, and guide us to lead with humility and love. Teach us to see every task as an opportunity to serve You and Your people. May our leadership reflect Your servant heart and bear witness to the hope of Your kingdom. Amen.

Day 11

"But those who hope in the Lord will renew their strength; they will fly up on wings like eagles; they will run and not be tired; they will walk and not be weary."

— Isaiah 40:31 (CEB)

Reflection

Leadership in the church is demanding. The weight of decisions, the strain of limited resources, the heartache of conflict, and the endless cycle of tasks can leave even the most faithful leaders weary. Isaiah's words come as a promise: those who place their hope in the Lord will find renewal, strength, and endurance that do not come from themselves but from God's Spirit.

Hope is more than optimism. It is trust in God's sustaining presence. Leaders often attempt to push through fatigue on their own, relying on determination or duty. Yet Isaiah reminds us that true renewal does not come from sheer willpower but from waiting on God. Renewal requires surrender, pausing long enough to release burdens and receive strength that only the Spirit can provide.

This renewal is essential for personal leadership. Treasurers who carry the responsibility of financial stewardship need more than spreadsheets to sustain them; they need hope in God's provision. Pastors who pour themselves into preaching, vision, and care cannot rely only on their own energy; they must draw from God's well of strength. Chairs who guide groups through conflict require more than patience; they require the Spirit's renewing peace. Officers and lay leaders who serve faithfully in quiet roles need assurance that their work matters and that God is with them. Without renewal, leaders burn out. With renewal, they can walk, run, and soar again.

Renewal is also essential for communal leadership. Churches, like leaders, can grow weary. Congregations may become discouraged by declining attendance, financial strain, or cultural pressures. Leaders who place their hope in God model for their communities what it looks like to find strength beyond circumstance. When leaders lead from renewal, they invite the entire body into rhythms of rest, prayer, and hope. They remind the church that it is God's Spirit, not human striving, that sustains the mission.

Spirit-led stewardship grows from this posture of hope. Leaders who are renewed by God are less likely to lead out of fear or scarcity. Instead, they can lead with courage, generosity, and trust. Renewal allows leaders to see beyond immediate challenges to the deeper purposes of God at work. It gives perspective, grounding leadership not in exhaustion but in faith.

There is a paradox in this promise. Renewal comes not by doing more, but by waiting—by resting, by trusting, by hoping. It is counterintuitive in a world that values constant productivity. Yet it is precisely this countercultural rhythm that equips leaders to endure. Like eagles soaring on thermals, leaders who hope in God are carried by strength not their own.

Isaiah does not promise that the work will become easy or that challenges will vanish. He promises that those who hope in the Lord will not be crushed by weariness. They will be able to keep going, sustained by a source greater than themselves.

As leaders, we must continually return to this promise. Renewal is not a luxury; it is part of our calling. To lead faithfully is to lead from a place of strength renewed by God.

Application

Take ten minutes today to step away from your tasks. Sit in silence, read Isaiah 40:31 slowly, and invite God to renew your strength. Write down one area of your leadership where you feel most weary. Then write a prayer of release, offering it to God and trusting that the Spirit will sustain you. If you are with others, share your reflections and pray for one another's renewal.

_____

_____

_____

_____

_____

_____

_____

_____

Prayer

God of strength and hope, we confess our weariness. Too often we rely on our own power and lose sight of Your presence. Renew us by Your Spirit. Lift us on wings like eagles, that we may run without growing tired and walk without losing heart. Teach us to lead from Your strength, not our own, and to model renewal for the communities we serve. Amen.

Day 12

"The Lord is my shepherd, I lack nothing.
He makes me lie down in green pastures,
he leads me beside quiet waters,
he refreshes my soul.
He guides me along the right paths
for his name's sake."

— Psalm 23:1–3 (NIV)

Reflection

Psalm 23 paints a picture of God as the Shepherd who provides rest, refreshment, and guidance. For leaders in the church, these verses are not just comforting words—they are a vital reminder that leadership cannot be sustained without renewal. Just as sheep cannot thrive without the care of a shepherd, leaders cannot endure without allowing God to restore their souls.

Leadership often feels like constant movement—meetings to prepare, sermons to write, finances to balance, decisions to make. In the rush of responsibilities, it can feel indulgent, even irresponsible, to pause. Yet the Shepherd insists: *"He makes me lie down... He leads me beside quiet waters... He refreshes my soul."* Renewal is not optional. It is part of God's care for those entrusted with the weight of leadership.

For treasurers, renewal may come in trusting that financial pressures are not borne alone, but are carried in prayer and shared with the community. For pastors, renewal may mean stepping away from endless tasks to receive the stillness of God's presence. For chairs, renewal may mean remembering that guiding a board does not depend solely on their wisdom, but on God's leading. For officers and lay leaders, renewal may mean recognizing that even behind-the-scenes service is seen and sustained by God.

Personal renewal strengthens communal leadership. Congregations led by weary, depleted leaders often mirror that weariness. But when leaders draw from the Shepherd's refreshment, they can guide communities with peace, patience, and resilience. Renewal allows leaders to bring a non-anxious presence into anxious spaces, reminding the church through their own lives that God provides what is needed.

This psalm also reminds us that renewal is not only about rest, but about direction. *"He guides me along the right paths for his name's sake."* Renewal equips leaders not only to keep going, but to move faithfully in the right direction. Discernment and guidance come more clearly when leaders allow their souls to be restored.

Spirit-led stewardship is rooted in this rhythm of renewal. Leaders are entrusted with people, resources, and mission, but they are also entrusted with their own wellbeing. To neglect rest is to neglect stewardship of the very vessel God has chosen to lead. To embrace rest and renewal is to honor God's gift of leadership and to acknowledge our dependence on the Shepherd.

It is worth noticing that the psalm begins with trust: *"The Lord is my shepherd, I lack nothing."* Renewal begins not with effort but with trust. Leaders are called to release the illusion of self-sufficiency and lean into the Shepherd's care. Renewal is God's work in us, not our achievement.

As leaders reflect on this psalm, they are invited to remember that their calling does not require constant striving. It requires faithful trust in the One who restores, refreshes, and guides. Renewal is not weakness; it is the very foundation that sustains leadership for the long journey.

Application

Set aside a moment today to pray Psalm 23:1–3 slowly, imagining yourself resting in green pastures and walking beside quiet waters. Write down one way you sense God refreshing your soul. If you are with others, share what renewal looks like in your leadership and ask: *How can we as a group encourage one another to rest in God's care?*

_____

_____

_____

_____

_____

_____

_____

_____

Prayer

Shepherding God, You lead us to places of rest and refreshment, even when we resist. Teach us to trust that we lack nothing in Your care. Restore our souls when we are weary, and guide us on right paths that honor Your name. Help us to lead from a place of renewal, so that our lives and our leadership bear witness to Your sustaining love. Amen.

Day 13

"Are you tired? Worn out? Burned out on religion? Come to me. Get away with me and you'll recover your life. I'll show you how to take a real rest. Walk with me and work with me—watch how I do it. Learn the unforced rhythms of grace. I won't lay anything heavy or ill-fitting on you. Keep company with me and you'll learn to live freely and lightly."

— Matthew 11:28–30 (MSG)

Reflection

Jesus' invitation to the weary is one of the most tender promises in all of Scripture. He does not ask us to pretend our exhaustion isn't real. He names it: *Are you tired? Worn out? Burned out?* For church leaders, these words often strike uncomfortably close. Leadership can stretch us thin—balancing budgets, preparing sermons, navigating conflict, making decisions, supporting others. Many leaders try to carry these responsibilities in their own strength until they feel spent.

Jesus' response is not to offer more strategies for efficiency, but to extend an invitation: *Come to me. Get away with me. Walk with me.* Renewal, he insists, is not found in doing more but in learning a new rhythm—the "unforced rhythms of grace."

For leaders, this requires a shift in perspective. We often measure ourselves by what we accomplish: the meetings chaired, the ministries launched, the budgets balanced. But Jesus reframes leadership as relationship. Renewal flows not from our pace of work but from our closeness to him. He promises that when we walk and work with him, the burdens we carry will not be crushing, because he will shoulder them with us.

This is not to say that leadership becomes easy. Jesus never promises a life without challenges. But he promises that his yoke is different—never heavy or ill-fitting. The tasks he entrusts to us are matched with the grace to bear them. The load may still be weighty, but it will not destroy us, because it is shared with him.

For treasurers, this may mean releasing the anxiety of numbers into Christ's hands and remembering that financial leadership is a ministry of trust. For pastors, it may mean pausing in prayer before rushing to respond, allowing the Spirit to set the pace. For chairs, it may mean guiding dialogue with patience rather than pressure, trusting that God's direction does not need to be forced. For officers and lay leaders, it may mean finding joy in quiet service, knowing that unseen faithfulness is precious in God's sight.

Communal renewal flows from leaders who embrace these rhythms. When leaders live freely and lightly, they model for the church that following Christ is not about constant strain but about resting in God's grace. Congregations led by anxious, burned-out leaders often mirror that anxiety.

But when leaders walk with Christ at a sustainable pace, they invite the entire community into renewal.

Spirit-led stewardship grows from this same rhythm. Leaders who walk in grace resist the urge to lead from fear or scarcity. Instead, they lead from trust, generosity, and peace. Stewardship of time, energy, and resources is no longer about squeezing out more effort but about aligning with the Spirit's flow.

The invitation of Jesus is not just for moments of crisis; it is for every day. Renewal is not a one-time retreat but a daily decision to walk with him, to learn his pace, and to trust his presence. When leaders accept this invitation, they discover that leadership does not have to drain them dry. Instead, it can become an expression of life lived in the rhythms of grace.

Application

Take a few minutes today to reflect on your current pace of leadership. Where are you pushing too hard, carrying too much, or moving faster than grace allows? Write down one way you can slow down and walk more closely with Jesus this week. If you are in a group, share your reflections and consider together: *What does it mean for our leadership to embody the "unforced rhythms of grace"?*

Prayer

Gentle Savior, You invite us to come to You when we are weary and worn. Teach us to walk in Your unforced rhythms of grace. Free us from the burdens we place on ourselves, and remind us that we are not alone in our work. Renew our strength, lighten our steps, and guide us to lead with peace, trust, and joy. Amen.

Day 14

"So let us not grow weary in doing what is right, for we will reap at harvest time, if we do not give up."

— Galatians 6:9 (NRSVue)

Reflection

Paul's encouragement to the Galatians is a reminder for all who labor in leadership: weariness is real, but it does not have to define us. Leadership in the church demands perseverance. It requires showing up for meetings, managing resources faithfully, shepherding people through joys and sorrows, and staying steady in seasons of uncertainty. Over time, this steady faithfulness can feel exhausting. Paul does not dismiss that reality. Instead, he points us to the promise of God's harvest if we do not give up.

Doing what is right is often the harder path. It is easier to avoid conflict than to engage it with truth and love. It is easier to protect personal comfort than to make decisions that serve the mission of the whole. It is easier to measure success by quick wins than to trust in the long work of transformation. Yet leadership rooted in Christ is not about ease but about faithfulness. It is about continuing to plant, water, and nurture—even when results are not immediately visible—trusting that God brings the harvest in God's time.

This promise is vital for personal renewal. Treasurers may not see gratitude for their hours of careful stewardship. Chairs may not always witness the fruit of facilitating honest dialogue. Pastors may preach or guide without clear evidence of change. Officers may serve faithfully with little recognition. Yet Paul insists: none of this labor is wasted. The Spirit is at work beneath the surface, and in God's time, fruit will appear.

Communal renewal flows from this same assurance. Congregations can grow weary, especially when challenges seem overwhelming or progress feels slow. Leaders who cling to the promise of harvest remind their communities that faithfulness is never in vain. By modeling perseverance with hope, leaders strengthen the body to endure and to trust that God's purposes will be fulfilled.

This call to perseverance does not mean leaders should ignore their own limits. Paul does not suggest that we must press forward by our own strength. Renewal comes when we ground our hope not in ourselves but in God. When leaders pause to rest, pray, and reconnect with the Spirit, they find strength to keep going without burning out. Renewal is not the opposite of perseverance; it is the very practice that allows perseverance to continue.

Spirit-led stewardship grows from this posture. Leaders are entrusted with responsibilities that may not bear fruit immediately. Stewardship means tending faithfully, even in seasons of apparent barrenness, knowing that the harvest is God's to bring. It also means creating space for rest and renewal so that our labor can remain steady over the long journey.

As you reflect on these words, remember that leadership is not about quick results but about faithfulness over time. You may not always see the fruit of your work. But if you remain steadfast, God promises a harvest that will reveal the depth of your calling and the richness of your service.

Application

Write down one area of your leadership where you feel weary or tempted to give up. Reflect on what it would look like to trust God with the timing of the harvest in that area. If you are in a group, share your reflections and encourage one another with stories of perseverance, asking together: *Where do we see signs of God's harvest beginning to grow?*

_____

_____

_____

_____

_____

_____

_____

_____

_____

Prayer

God of promise and endurance, You see our weariness and You know our struggles. Renew our strength so that we may not give up in doing what is right. Teach us to trust that the seeds we plant in faith will bear fruit in Your time. Keep us steady in our calling, and grant us the joy of seeing Your harvest of love, justice, and peace. Amen.

Day 15

"Being always full of the joy of the Lord, and always strong and vigorous in the strength of his glorious power, so you can keep going no matter what happens—always full of the joy of the Lord, and always thankful to the Father who has made us fit to share all the wonderful things that belong to those who live in the Kingdom of light."

— Colossians 1:11–12 (TLB)

Reflection

Paul's prayer for the believers in Colossae speaks directly to the heart of every leader who has felt worn down by the weight of ministry. He does not simply wish them endurance—he prays that they will be strengthened with God's glorious power, filled with joy, and rooted in gratitude. Renewal, Paul suggests, is not a fleeting moment of relief but a steady way of living, grounded in God's strength rather than our own.

Leadership often requires resilience in the face of challenge. Treasurers bear the responsibility of stewarding limited resources with wisdom. Chairs hold the tension of guiding difficult conversations while keeping the mission central. Pastors pour themselves into preaching, care, and vision, often giving more than they think they have. Officers and lay leaders serve with constancy, sometimes without recognition. These responsibilities can wear leaders down if carried alone. But Paul reminds us that God's glorious power supplies the strength we cannot generate ourselves.

Notice how Paul frames this strength: it is not merely endurance, but endurance filled with joy. Joy is not the absence of struggle; it is the presence of God's Spirit in the midst of it. Joy renews us when circumstances weigh us down. It shifts our focus from what is lacking to the abundance of God's presence. Leaders who cultivate joy are not ignoring hardship but are choosing to see God's gifts even in the midst of difficulty.

Gratitude plays a central role in this renewal. Paul insists that leaders remain "thankful to the Father." Gratitude reframes leadership from a burdensome task to a sacred trust. It helps leaders see meetings not only as obligations but as opportunities to discern together. It allows treasurers to see financial reports as testimonies of faith. It enables pastors to see the small acts of faithfulness in their congregation as signs of God's Kingdom. Gratitude lifts leaders beyond discouragement, anchoring them in the reality of God's generosity.

Communal renewal flows when leaders embody joy and gratitude together. Congregations are deeply influenced by the spirit of their leaders. A community led by exhausted, resentful leaders often reflects that spirit. But when leaders demonstrate gratitude and joy, they remind the church that its life is sustained not by scarcity or fear but by the abundance of God's power. Renewal is not only personal; it becomes a gift the whole community receives through the posture of its leaders.

Spirit-led stewardship grows from this foundation. To lead with strength rooted in God, with joy that springs from the Spirit, and with gratitude that acknowledges God's generosity is to steward leadership faithfully. Leaders who embrace this way of living can "keep going no matter what happens," as Paul prays, because they know the source of their renewal is inexhaustible.

As you reflect today, remember that burnout is not inevitable. Renewal is possible when leaders release the illusion of self-sufficiency and lean into the joy, strength, and gratitude that God provides.

Application

Reflect on one area of your leadership where you feel drained. Write down one reason for gratitude you can identify in that very area—something that points to God's presence, even if small. If you are with a group, share your reflections and ask: *How can joy and gratitude sustain us as leaders, even when challenges persist?*

_____

_____

_____

_____

_____

_____

_____

_____

Prayer

God of glorious power, thank You for giving us strength beyond our own. Fill us with the joy of Your Spirit and the gratitude that flows from knowing we belong to Your Kingdom. Renew us when we are weary, and help us to keep going with courage, humility, and hope. May our leadership reflect Your abundance and invite others to trust in Your sustaining love. Amen.

Day 16

"I can do all this through Christ, who gives me strength."

— Philippians 4:13 (CEV)

Reflection

Few verses have been quoted more often by weary leaders than Paul's declaration to the Philippians. It is not a boast of self-sufficiency but a testimony of reliance. Paul writes these words from prison, stripped of freedom and surrounded by uncertainty, yet he proclaims confidence—not in his own ability, but in Christ who supplies strength.

Leadership in the church requires this same reliance. The demands are relentless: treasurers balancing budgets in seasons of scarcity, pastors preaching hope amid discouragement, chairs guiding meetings that carry heavy decisions, officers serving faithfully even when unnoticed. Each role carries burdens that can easily overwhelm. Left to our own resources, burnout is inevitable. But Paul reminds us that leadership is not sustained by human effort alone. Christ himself strengthens us for the work.

This strength is not a surge of adrenaline or a fleeting burst of energy. It is the quiet, steady resilience that comes from Christ's presence. It allows leaders to rise after disappointment, to endure through conflict, to remain faithful when results are not visible. It is the strength that keeps treasurers focused when numbers don't add up, that steadies pastors when sermons feel dry, that equips chairs to listen more than speak, and that helps officers continue serving with grace.

Personal renewal begins here: recognizing that leadership is not about carrying the weight alone but about sharing it with Christ. Too often, leaders mistake self-reliance for faithfulness, pushing themselves harder and harder until exhaustion sets in. But Paul teaches us that true faithfulness comes from surrender. To admit our need for Christ's strength is not weakness—it is the very source of renewal.

Communal renewal flows from leaders who embody this dependence. Congregations notice when leaders attempt to lead from their own power, often reflecting the anxiety or frustration that results. But when leaders model reliance on Christ, they invite the whole body to trust God's sustaining grace. They remind the church that its mission does not rest on a few shoulders but on the strength of Christ who holds the whole body together.

Spirit-led stewardship grows out of this posture of trust. Leaders are called to steward not only finances, programs, and people but also their own capacity. To ignore limits is to risk collapse. To acknowledge dependence on Christ is to practice stewardship of the most essential resource: the Spirit's sustaining presence. This shifts leadership from striving to trusting, from burnout to renewal, from fear to hope.

Paul's words are not permission to attempt everything. They are a reminder that whatever Christ calls us to, Christ will also equip us for. Leaders may not be able to fix every problem or carry every burden, but they can trust that Christ will give them strength for the tasks God has placed before them. That promise is enough to keep going when leadership feels overwhelming, and it is enough to guard us from despair when progress feels slow.

As you reflect today, hear Paul's declaration not as a demand for superhuman effort, but as a reminder of Christ's nearness. You are not asked to do everything, but you are promised strength for what you are called to do.

Application

Reflect on one area of leadership where you feel weakest or most drained. Write it down, and beside it write Paul's words: *"I can do all this through Christ, who gives me strength."* Pray over that area, asking Christ to supply the strength you cannot provide yourself. If you are with a group, share your reflections and ask: *Where do we most need to rely on Christ's strength together?*

_____

_____

_____

_____

_____

_____

Prayer

Strength-giving Christ, we confess that too often we try to lead in our own power. Teach us to rely on You, to draw our renewal from Your presence, and to trust that You will sustain us. Strengthen us in weakness, calm us in weariness, and guide us in hope. May our leadership reflect not our striving but Your grace, so that all we do bears witness to Your power and love. Amen.

Day 17

"Unless the Lord builds the house, the builders labor in vain. Unless the Lord watches over the city, the guards stand watch in vain."

— Psalm 127:1 (NIV)

Reflection

This psalm reminds leaders of a truth that is both humbling and liberating: all our work is meaningless unless it is rooted in God's presence and purpose. Leadership in the church demands diligence, but it also requires surrender. When we attempt to carry the mission by ourselves—relying only on human wisdom, effort, and control—we risk burnout. Renewal begins when we remember that the work belongs to God first.

Church leadership is often marked by long hours, difficult decisions, and the temptation to measure success by visible results. Treasurers may feel pressure to make every dollar stretch further. Pastors may shoulder the expectation of growth and inspiration week after week. Chairs may wrestle with conflicting opinions and the responsibility of holding the group steady. Officers may quietly sustain ministries without recognition. Each of these roles matters deeply, but none can thrive apart from God's sustaining presence.

The psalmist insists that unless God is the one building, our labor is in vain. This does not mean leaders should abandon planning, effort, or attention to detail. It means that our work must flow from trust in God's initiative, not from anxiety about our own performance. Renewal comes when leaders release the burden of ultimate responsibility and remember that they are stewards, not owners, of the work.

This truth speaks into communal leadership as well. Congregations sometimes place unrealistic expectations on leaders, as though their skill or charisma alone will guarantee the church's future. But just as builders cannot raise a house without God, leaders cannot sustain a church's life apart from God's presence. When leaders guide their communities to trust that God is the builder, they model faith over fear, hope over exhaustion.

Spirit-led stewardship emerges from this posture of dependence. Treasurers, when they interpret budgets as instruments of faith rather than scarcity, help the community see that resources belong to God. Pastors, when they lead from prayer rather than pressure, remind the church that vision arises from God's Spirit. Chairs, when they foster discernment instead of debate, open the way for God's direction to be heard. Officers, when they serve with quiet faithfulness, bear witness to God's sustaining hand. In each role, the key is not control but surrender—recognizing that the work is God's before it is ours.

Burnout often comes from forgetting this truth. Leaders take on more than they were meant to carry, convinced that everything depends on them. But when leaders rest in God's presence, they find freedom to let go of perfectionism and to lead with trust. Renewal is found not in doing less work but in remembering whose work it is.

This psalm calls us back to humility: we are builders and watchmen, but the house and city belong to the Lord. It also calls us to hope: God is the true builder and guardian, and our labor is never wasted when it flows from God's purpose. Renewal comes in this balance—working faithfully, while resting in the assurance that God is the one who sustains.

Application

Reflect on an area of your leadership where you feel the pressure to carry too much on your own. Write down the phrase: *"Unless the Lord builds the house, the builders labor in vain."* Pray over this area, releasing control to God. If you are with a group, invite each leader to name one part of their role they need to entrust more fully to God's care.

_____

_____

_____

_____

_____

_____

_____

_____

_____

Prayer

God our Builder and Guardian, forgive us when we try to carry the weight of leadership on our own. Teach us to trust that the work is Yours before it is ours. Renew us with the assurance that You are building and watching, even when we cannot see the full picture. Strengthen our hands to serve faithfully, and calm our hearts to rest in Your sustaining presence. Amen.

Day 18

"But we have this treasure in clay pots so that the awesome power belongs to God and doesn't come from us. We are experiencing all kinds of trouble, but we aren't crushed. We are confused, but we aren't depressed. We are harassed, but we aren't abandoned. We are knocked down, but we aren't knocked out."

— 2 Corinthians 4:7–9 (CEB)

Reflection

Paul's image of clay pots holding a priceless treasure speaks directly to the experience of church leadership. Clay is fragile, easily chipped or broken, yet within it rests something of infinite worth. Leaders, too, often feel their own limits. They carry responsibilities that seem heavier than their strength, face challenges that expose their vulnerabilities, and encounter seasons of discouragement. Yet Paul reminds us that the treasure is not diminished by the weakness of the vessel. The power belongs to God, not to us.

For treasurers, the fragility may show up in the stress of balancing limited resources. For pastors, it may come through the weariness of constant preaching, care, and vision. For chairs, it may appear in the strain of guiding difficult conversations. For officers and lay leaders, it may take the form of unnoticed but necessary service. Each leader knows the feeling of being stretched thin, of wondering whether their vessel can hold. Yet in these very moments, God's power is revealed most clearly.

Paul does not deny hardship. He names it: trouble, confusion, harassment, being knocked down. Burnout often grows when leaders feel they must hide or minimize these struggles. But renewal comes when we can acknowledge our weakness honestly, trusting that it does not disqualify us from leadership but opens the way for God's strength to shine through.

This perspective reshapes how we lead. We are not called to prove ourselves as unbreakable, but to point to the treasure within. Leadership is not about showing perfect strength but about embodying faithful reliance. The community does not need flawless leaders; it needs leaders who remind them that God's power is greater than human frailty.

Communal renewal grows from this truth. When leaders model vulnerability and trust, congregations are freed from the illusion that faith requires perfection. They see that the church itself—fragile in many ways—carries within it the treasure of the gospel. Leaders who admit their weariness, yet testify to God's sustaining presence, teach the whole body that resilience is not self-made but Spirit-given.

Spirit-led stewardship also flows from this understanding. To steward leadership as a clay pot is to care for our limits, to rest when needed, and to resist the temptation to carry more than God has given us. It is also to remember that what we hold—God's grace, God's mission, God's people—is a treasure. Even in fragile hands, the gospel shines.

Paul's closing words offer resilience: "We are knocked down, but we aren't knocked out." Leaders will stumble. They will face discouragement and even failure. Yet the promise of God's power means that no setback is final. Renewal comes not from avoiding hardship but from trusting that God will lift us up again and again.

As you reflect today, remember that your fragility is not a flaw to be hidden but a truth to be embraced. You are a clay pot carrying a treasure beyond price. And that treasure—the presence and power of God—will never fail.

Application

Write down one area of your leadership where you feel most fragile right now. Then write beside it: *"The treasure belongs to God, not to me."* Reflect on how this truth reframes your sense of weakness. If you are with a group, share your reflections and encourage one another by naming the ways God's power has been revealed in your fragile moments.

_____

_____

_____

_____

_____

_____

_____

_____

Prayer

God of power and grace, we confess our fragility. We are often weary, confused, and knocked down. Yet we thank You that Your treasure shines through our weakness. Teach us to lead with honesty, to trust Your strength in our limits, and to find renewal in Your sustaining presence. May our lives and our leadership point always to Your glory, not our own. Amen.

Day 19

"Jesus said, 'The food that keeps me going is that I do the will of the One who sent me, finishing the work he started.'"

— John 4:34 (MSG)

Reflection

Jesus' words to his disciples in John 4 come after a moment of physical weariness. Hungry and thirsty, he pauses at a well. Yet when the disciples urge him to eat, he explains that his true sustenance comes not from bread but from doing the will of God. This perspective offers profound wisdom for leaders who often struggle with exhaustion and burnout: renewal is not only found in rest but in re-centering on God's mission.

Leaders give much of themselves in service—time, energy, wisdom, and emotional presence. It is easy to feel depleted when the demands outweigh visible results. But Jesus reminds us that there is a kind of nourishment that comes from alignment with God's will. To know that our leadership, however ordinary or hidden, is part of God's ongoing work provides strength deeper than physical energy.

For treasurers, this might mean recognizing that financial stewardship is not just about numbers but about enabling the church to live its mission. For pastors, it might mean remembering that preaching and care are not ends in themselves but acts of participating in God's work of transformation. For chairs, it might mean seeing the work of facilitating meetings not as drudgery but as guiding the community to discern God's path. For officers and lay leaders, it might mean trusting that their quiet, faithful presence is part of God's sustaining grace for the church.

When leaders reframe their tasks as participation in God's will, the work itself can become a source of renewal. This does not mean ignoring the need for physical rest or emotional care. Jesus himself withdrew often to pray and recharge. But it does mean that energy is replenished when we reconnect with the deeper purpose of our calling. The food that keeps us going is not merely success or recognition—it is the joy of knowing we are aligned with God's mission.

Communal renewal flows from this perspective as well. Congregations can lose sight of purpose, becoming weighed down by maintenance or discouraged by challenges. Leaders who stay rooted in God's mission remind the body of its true nourishment. They call the community to look beyond survival toward the joy of participating in God's work. Such leadership brings life and focus to the whole church.

Spirit-led stewardship grows naturally from this alignment. Leaders who see their work as service to God's mission are less likely to lead from anxiety or self-interest. Instead, they steward their time, gifts, and responsibilities with trust and hope. They are renewed not only by what they accomplish but by who they serve.

This passage challenges us to ask: what truly sustains us as leaders? If we rely only on external affirmation, visible results, or personal strength, burnout is near. But if we allow the will of God to be our nourishment, then even in seasons of difficulty we can find renewal. The Spirit reminds us that the work is not ours to finish alone—it is God's work, and we are invited to take part.

As you reflect today, remember that leadership is not about carrying everything on your shoulders. It is about being sustained by the One who calls and equips you. The food that keeps you going is not your own effort but the joy of joining in God's ongoing mission.

Application

Reflect on a leadership task that feels most draining for you right now. Write it down, and then ask: *How is this part of God's ongoing work?* Reframe the task as participation in God's mission, and pray for the Spirit to renew you through that alignment. If you are with others, share your reflections and ask: *What gives us energy as we join in God's work together?*

_____

_____

_____

_____

_____

_____

Prayer

God of mission and renewal, we thank You for sustaining us not only with rest but with purpose. Remind us that our true nourishment comes from doing Your will and joining in the work You began. When we feel weary, renew us with joy in serving You. Teach us to see every task as part of Your mission, and strengthen us to keep going with gratitude and hope. Amen.

Day 20

"Therefore, since we are surrounded by so great a cloud of witnesses, let us also lay aside every weight and the sin that clings so closely, and let us run with perseverance the race that is set before us, looking to Jesus, the pioneer and perfecter of faith, who for the sake of the joy that was set before him endured the cross, disregarding its shame, and has taken his seat at the right hand of the throne of God."

— Hebrews 12:1–2 (NRSVue)

Reflection

The image of running a race is a powerful one for leaders who often feel the strain of endurance. Leadership in the church is not a sprint. It is a marathon marked by long seasons of responsibility, moments of weariness, and the constant temptation to give up. The writer of Hebrews offers encouragement: you are not running alone. You are surrounded by a great cloud of witnesses, cheered on by those who have gone before, and strengthened by Christ who leads the way.

Renewal comes when leaders remember that they are part of this larger story. You are not carrying the mission alone. Others have run before you, and others will come after you. Treasurers, pastors, chairs, officers, and lay leaders all share in this long race, each contributing their gifts to the work of God's kingdom. The cloud of witnesses reminds us that faithfulness, not speed, is what matters most.

The passage also calls us to lay aside the weights that slow us down. For leaders, these weights might be perfectionism, fear of failure, or the need for constant control. They may be resentments carried from past conflicts, or the burden of trying to please everyone. Renewal requires releasing these weights, trusting that the race is not won by carrying more but by carrying less—running light, running free, running with focus on Christ.

Perseverance is not the same as exhaustion. It is not grinding forward at any cost. Perseverance, in the vision of Hebrews, is sustained by joy. Jesus endured the cross "for the sake of the joy set before him." That joy—the joy of fulfilling God's will, the joy of resurrection hope—carried him through suffering. Leaders too can find strength in joy: the joy of seeing lives changed, of witnessing generosity, of sharing Christ's love in small but significant ways. Renewal is found in remembering the joy that makes endurance possible.

The writer points us finally to Jesus, the pioneer and perfecter of faith. Renewal is not about fixing our eyes on ourselves—our own performance, our own weariness, our own doubts—but on Christ. He has gone ahead of us, showing us how to run faithfully, and he remains with us, sustaining us as we run. Leaders who fix their eyes on Christ find perspective: their labor is not in vain, their struggles are not ultimate, their hope is secure.

Communal renewal grows when leaders embrace this perspective together. Congregations need leaders who model perseverance rooted in hope, not in frantic striving. When leaders run with joy and focus, the whole church learns to do the same. Together, they bear witness to a way of life that is steady, resilient, and sustained by God's Spirit.

Application

Reflect on one "weight" that slows you down in leadership—perhaps perfectionism, resentment, or fear. Write it down, and offer it to God in prayer, asking for the freedom to run with perseverance. If you are with others, invite each person to name what weight they long to release, and encourage one another by fixing your shared focus on Christ, the pioneer and perfecter of faith.

_____

_____

_____

_____

_____

_____

_____

_____

_____

_____

_____

Prayer

God of endurance and joy, thank You for surrounding us with a cloud of witnesses who remind us that we do not run alone. Help us to lay aside the weights that burden us and to run with perseverance the race You have set before us. Fix our eyes on Jesus, who leads and sustains us. Renew our strength, restore our joy, and guide us to lead with hope that endures. Amen.

Day 21

"Anyone who manages the little he has been given with faithfulness and integrity will be trusted with more."

— Luke 16:10 (TLB)

Reflection

Jesus' teaching in this verse reminds leaders that stewardship is not only about grand gestures or significant resources—it begins with the small things. Faithfulness in what may seem ordinary or unnoticed is the foundation for greater responsibility. For church leaders, this truth has profound implications for how we view our time, talents, and assets.

Time is one of the most precious resources entrusted to us. Leaders often feel pulled in countless directions, with calendars that never seem to have enough space. Stewarding time faithfully means recognizing that each moment is a gift from God, meant to be ordered with intention. Faithfulness in time is not about filling every hour with activity, but about aligning priorities with God's call. Sometimes stewardship means saying "yes" to presence and prayer, and sometimes it means saying "no" to demands that distract from mission.

Talents, too, are entrusted for the sake of others. A treasurer's attention to detail, a pastor's gift for vision, a chair's ability to guide dialogue, and an officer's faithfulness in service—each of these gifts, when offered with integrity, builds up the body of Christ. Yet talents are not meant to be hoarded or hidden. Stewardship requires cultivating them, sharing them, and using them for the good of the community. Faithfulness with our talents means offering them generously, trusting that God can multiply even what feels small.

Assets, whether financial or material, are also part of the trust God has placed in leaders. The Ministry of Money reminds us that stewardship is not merely bookkeeping but a spiritual practice. The way a church handles its resources tells a story about its trust in God and its commitment to mission. Leaders are called to ensure that assets are managed with transparency, integrity, and generosity—not for self-preservation, but for the flourishing of God's work. Faithfulness with financial resources means asking not just, "Is this sustainable?" but also, "Does this reflect God's mission?"

This verse also speaks to the communal dimension of stewardship. When leaders model faithfulness with time, talents, and assets, they shape a culture of trust within the congregation. Members learn that every gift matters, no matter how small. A small act of service, a modest offering, or a few minutes given in prayer—each is part of the whole, and each is seen by

God. Communities that honor small faithfulness are often the ones most prepared for larger opportunities.

Burnout often occurs when leaders confuse faithfulness with doing everything. Jesus does not call us to carry more than we are entrusted with. He calls us to steward well what we have been given. Faithfulness in small things is not about overwork; it is about integrity, consistency, and trust. Renewal comes when leaders release the pressure of comparison and embrace the truth that their call is not to do everything but to do faithfully what is theirs to do.

As leaders reflect on this passage, they are reminded that stewardship is not about control but about trust. Faithfulness with what we have now prepares us for what God may entrust to us in the future. The road to greater responsibility begins with integrity in the present moment.

Application

Identify one area of leadership—time, talent, or assets—where you are tempted to overlook the small things. Write down one specific way you can practice faithfulness in that area this week. If you are with a group, share your reflections and ask together: *What does faithfulness in the "little things" look like for our congregation, and how might it prepare us for more?*

_____

_____

_____

_____

_____

_____

_____

Prayer

Faithful God, You have entrusted us with time, talents, and resources, both great and small. Teach us to steward each gift with integrity, gratitude, and care. Free us from the temptation to overlook the ordinary, and help us to see how even small acts of faithfulness serve Your mission. Strengthen us to lead with trust, that our stewardship may bear fruit for Your kingdom and reflect Your generosity to the world. Amen.

Day 22

"Remember this saying, 'A few seeds make a small harvest, but a lot of seeds make a big harvest.' Each of you must make up your own mind about how much to give. But don't feel sorry that you must give and don't feel forced to give—God loves people who love to give. God can bless you with everything you need, and you will always have more than enough to do all kinds of good things for others."

— 2 Corinthians 9:6–8 (CEV)

Reflection

Paul's teaching to the Corinthians frames stewardship not as a matter of obligation but as an act of joy and trust. Giving—whether of time, talents, or assets—is not about meeting quotas or checking boxes. It is about sowing seeds generously, trusting that God will multiply them into a harvest of blessing for the community and beyond.

This image of sowing speaks to every leader in the church. Treasurers steward resources with care, ensuring that funds are used wisely to further the mission. Pastors sow seeds through preaching, prayer, and presence, trusting that the Spirit will bring growth. Chairs sow seeds by fostering healthy conversations and guiding decisions that build trust. Officers and lay leaders sow seeds of service, often in small, quiet ways that sustain the body. Each act of giving—financial, practical, spiritual—is a seed that contributes to God's harvest.

The key, Paul insists, is the spirit in which we give. Stewardship done reluctantly or under compulsion drains life from both giver and receiver. But when giving flows from love, gratitude, and joy, it becomes life-giving. Leaders are called to embody this spirit of generosity, not only in financial stewardship but in how they offer their time and talents. When leaders model joy in giving, they help congregations see stewardship not as a burden but as a privilege.

Generosity also counters the fear of scarcity that so often drives burnout in leadership. Leaders may worry there will never be enough—enough money to fund ministry, enough time to manage responsibilities, enough volunteers to sustain programs. Paul reframes the conversation: God is able to bless abundantly, providing "more than enough" to do the good works set before us. Stewardship rooted in trust transforms fear into freedom. Instead of clinging tightly to resources, leaders can open their hands, confident that God provides.

Communal discernment grows from this posture of generosity. When boards and committees make decisions from a place of trust, they are more willing to invest in mission rather than retreat in fear. They can see financial resources not only as constraints but as opportunities to serve. They can recognize time and talent not as things to be hoarded but as gifts to be shared. A generous spirit shifts the culture of the church, allowing it to reflect the abundance of God's kingdom.

Spirit-led stewardship means holding all that we have—our hours, our skills, our money—as gifts entrusted by God. Leaders are not asked to do everything or give everything, but to give freely, joyfully, and faithfully. In doing so, they discover that stewardship is not about depletion but about renewal. As Paul promises, God supplies what we need and more, equipping us for every good work.

As you reflect today, remember that your leadership is not only about managing what is scarce but about sowing generously. Every act of faithful stewardship—large or small—is a seed in God's field. And God is faithful to bring the harvest.

Application

Reflect on one area of your leadership—time, talent, or assets—where you tend to give sparingly out of fear of scarcity. Write down one way you could sow more generously this week, trusting that God will provide what you need. If you are with others, share your reflections and ask: *What seeds of generosity is God calling our community to plant together?*

_____

_____

_____

_____

_____

_____

_____

_____

Prayer

Generous God, You are the source of every gift. Free us from fear and teach us to give with joy. Help us to see our time, talents, and resources not as our own possessions but as seeds entrusted to us for Your mission. Bless our giving so that it bears fruit in abundance, renewing us and strengthening our communities for every good work. Amen.

Day 23

"Honor the Lord with your wealth, with the firstfruits of all your crops; then your barns will be filled to overflowing, and your vats will brim over with new wine."

— Proverbs 3:9–10 (NIV)

Reflection

The wisdom of Proverbs teaches us that stewardship begins with honoring God. To give the "firstfruits" means to offer not what is left over, but what comes first—our best, not our scraps. This principle reaches far beyond money. It speaks to how we steward time, talents, and all that God has entrusted to us.

For church leaders, this call is both personal and communal. Personally, it challenges us to examine what we give to God from our own lives. Do we offer the first moments of our time, or only what is left after other demands are met? Do we use our talents in ways that serve God's mission, or only in ways that serve ourselves? Do we manage resources entrusted to us with integrity, or allow them to be shaped by fear and scarcity? Honoring God with the firstfruits is an invitation to put God at the center of everything we offer.

Communally, this wisdom reminds the church that stewardship is an act of collective witness. A congregation that gives its best to God—its best time, its best energy, its best resources—declares to the world that God is worthy of honor. A church that offers leftovers, by contrast, sends the message that God is secondary. Leaders play a crucial role in shaping this culture, not only by managing resources faithfully but by modeling generosity and commitment themselves.

For treasurers, honoring God with the firstfruits means framing financial leadership as more than balancing budgets. It means interpreting numbers as stories of mission, ensuring that the church's spending reflects its priorities of worship, service, and care. For pastors, it means preparing sermons and vision with attentiveness to God's call rather than rushing to fill obligations. For chairs, it means guiding meetings in ways that give priority to prayer and discernment before diving into business. For officers and lay leaders, it means showing up faithfully and offering service not as an afterthought but as a sacred act.

The promise of Proverbs is that when we honor God with our first and best, God provides abundantly. This is not a formula for material prosperity, but a testimony of trust. When leaders and congregations release their grip on resources and give generously, they discover that God's abundance meets their needs. The barns filled and vats brimming over are images of sufficiency and joy that flow from faithful stewardship.

This principle also offers renewal. Burnout often comes when leaders give endlessly without grounding their service in God's abundance. Honoring God with our firstfruits reorients us: leadership is not about draining ourselves dry, but about offering our best in trust that God will supply what we lack. When leaders give from gratitude rather than obligation, their stewardship becomes life-giving rather than exhausting.

Ultimately, stewardship is not about how much we have but about how we honor God with what we have. The invitation is to live and lead in a way that places God first, trusting that God's provision is enough for the journey.

Application

Reflect on one area of your leadership—time, talents, or assets—where you may be offering God what is left over instead of your best. Write down one concrete step you can take to give your firstfruits in that area. If you are with a group, invite one another to share reflections and ask together: *How can our congregation honor God with our first and best?*

_____

_____

_____

_____

_____

_____

_____

_____

_____

Prayer

Generous God, You are worthy of our first and best. Forgive us when we offer only what is left over. Teach us to honor You with our time, our talents, and our resources, trusting that You will provide abundantly for all we need. Renew our joy in stewardship, and let our leadership be a living testimony of gratitude, generosity, and trust in Your overflowing grace. Amen.

Day 24

"The kingdom of heaven is like a man who was leaving on a trip. He called his servants and handed his possessions over to them. To one he gave five valuable coins, and to another he gave two, and to another he gave one. He gave to each servant according to that servant's ability. Then he left on his journey."

— Matthew 25:14–15 (CEB)

Reflection

Jesus' parable of the talents, or valuable coins, offers a striking vision of stewardship. The master entrusts his possessions to his servants, not as a burden but as a responsibility that reflects trust. Each receives something of value, and each is expected to use what has been given faithfully. The story reminds leaders that all we manage—time, talents, and assets—are not ours by ownership but ours by trust.

Church leaders live this reality daily. Treasurers oversee financial resources, knowing they are not just numbers but sacred trusts meant for mission. Pastors steward the Word, vision, and care of the congregation. Chairs steward the order and integrity of leadership gatherings. Officers and lay leaders steward ministries, relationships, and the unseen work that keeps the church alive. In each role, God has entrusted something valuable, expecting leaders to use it for the flourishing of the community.

The master in the parable gives "according to ability." This is not favoritism but recognition of difference. Some are entrusted with much, others with less, but all are entrusted with something that matters. Faithful stewardship is not about comparing our portion to others but about using what we have been given. A treasurer may not preach. A pastor may not keep the books. A chair may not serve in quiet roles. But each has received a trust, and each is accountable for what they do with it.

This parable also challenges leaders to resist fear. One servant buries his coin, worried about risk and responsibility. How often do leaders do the same—playing it safe, avoiding decisions, or holding back gifts for fear of failure? Faithful stewardship is not about preservation but about participation. God calls leaders to invest their time, talents, and assets in ways that serve the kingdom. Playing it safe may feel secure, but it fails to honor the trust God has given.

At the same time, stewardship is not about reckless overextension. The parable reminds us that the master entrusts resources "according to ability." Renewal comes when leaders recognize their limits and steward accordingly. Burnout often arises when leaders try to carry more than what has been entrusted to them, or when they attempt to take on the responsibilities of others. Stewardship requires humility to focus on what is ours to carry and trust that others will carry what is theirs.

Communal stewardship grows when leaders encourage one another in this trust. The church flourishes when all gifts are recognized, honored, and used. A culture of stewardship is not built on envy or comparison but on gratitude—seeing each person's portion as part of the whole. When leaders affirm one another's contributions, they mirror the kingdom of heaven described in the parable: many trusts, many gifts, one mission.

Ultimately, this parable reminds us that what we have is not for ourselves but for God's purposes. Leadership stewardship is about asking: *How can my portion—whether large or small—serve the mission of Christ in this community?* The answer may look different for each role, but the calling is the same: to be faithful with what has been entrusted.

Application

Reflect on one "valuable coin" entrusted to you in your leadership role—whether time, talent, or resource. Write down how you are currently using it, and consider whether you are investing it fully or burying it in fear. If you are with a group, share your reflections and ask: *How can our leadership together ensure that all our gifts are invested for the sake of God's mission?*

_____

_____

_____

_____

_____

_____

_____

_____

_____

Prayer

Generous God, You have entrusted us with gifts, time, and resources for the sake of Your kingdom. Keep us from fear that buries what You have given, and teach us to invest with courage and faith. Help us honor the trust placed in us by leading with gratitude, wisdom, and hope. May our stewardship bear fruit for the life of the church and reflect Your abundance to the world. Amen.

Day 25

"Tell those rich in this world's wealth to quit being so full of themselves and so obsessed with money, which is here today and gone tomorrow. Tell them to go after God, who piles on all the riches we could ever manage—to do good, to be rich in helping others, to be extravagantly generous. If they do that, they'll build a treasury that will last, gaining life that is truly life."

— 1 Timothy 6:17–19 (MSG)

Reflection

Paul's words to Timothy remind us that stewardship is not about accumulation but about alignment. Wealth, time, and talents are temporary; they are entrusted to us for a season. The danger comes when leaders treat these gifts as possessions to protect rather than trusts to be used. Paul directs us to reframe our perspective: life that is truly life is found not in grasping but in giving.

For church leaders, this message strikes close to home. Treasurers, who manage the resources of the congregation, must balance careful oversight with the call to generosity. Pastors, who guide vision and mission, must remind communities that abundance is found in God's provision, not in financial security alone. Chairs, who facilitate decisions, must help groups resist fear-driven choices that prioritize preservation over purpose. Officers and lay leaders, who serve faithfully, embody stewardship when they give of themselves for the good of others. Each role carries the responsibility of helping the church use its resources—time, talents, and assets—in ways that reflect trust in God rather than anxiety about scarcity.

Paul urges generosity not as a burden but as a pathway to joy. To be "rich in helping others" is to recognize that our blessings are multiplied when shared. Leaders who embody this spirit remind congregations that stewardship is not simply about budgets or fundraising but about discipleship. It is about aligning our resources with God's mission so that lives may be transformed.

This passage also speaks to the communal dimension of stewardship. A congregation's culture is shaped by how its leaders talk about and model generosity. If leaders approach resources with fear, congregations will mirror that fear. If leaders treat stewardship as an obligation, congregations will do the same. But if leaders embody joy and gratitude in giving, they cultivate a culture of abundance where generosity flows naturally. Such a culture reflects the heart of God, who "piles on all the riches we could ever manage."

Spirit-led stewardship requires constant reorientation. Leaders must regularly ask: *Are we obsessed with protecting what we have, or are we pursuing God's mission with trust and boldness?* This does not mean recklessness. Wise stewardship includes accountability, transparency, and careful management. But wisdom also calls us to resist the temptation to hoard. The treasure

Paul describes is not stored in bank accounts but in lives touched, communities strengthened, and ministries empowered.

Burnout often comes when leaders measure themselves by numbers alone. When financial survival becomes the primary goal, leaders can lose sight of joy. Renewal comes when we recover Paul's vision of stewardship as participation in "life that is truly life." The measure of faithful leadership is not how much we preserve but how faithfully we release what we have for God's purposes.

As leaders reflect on this passage, they are invited to see every resource—whether time, talents, or assets—as part of God's abundance. Stewardship is not a task to dread but a calling to embody generosity that reflects the heart of Christ. Life that is truly life is discovered not in holding tightly but in giving freely.

Application

Reflect on one area of leadership where you are tempted to hold back—whether your time, a particular skill, or a resource under your care. Write down one way you could practice generosity in that area this week. If you are with a group, share your reflections and ask: *How can our leadership model generosity that leads to life that is truly life for our congregation?*

_____

_____

_____

_____

_____

_____

_____

Prayer

Generous God, You pour out blessings beyond measure. Forgive us when we cling to resources in fear or pride. Teach us to be rich in good works, faithful in sharing, and extravagant in generosity. Renew our joy in stewardship, and guide us to lead with open hands and grateful hearts. May our leadership reflect Your abundance and invite our communities into life that is truly life. Amen.

Day 26

"A generous person will be enriched, and one who gives water will get water."

— Proverbs 11:25 (NRSVue)

Reflection

The wisdom of Proverbs often teaches through paradox: in giving, we receive; in refreshing others, we ourselves are refreshed. This principle cuts against the grain of a culture that insists holding tightly is the surest way to survive. For church leaders, the lesson is clear—stewardship rooted in generosity is not depletion but renewal.

Generosity is not only about money. It includes time, talents, and every resource entrusted to us. Treasurers show generosity when they interpret financial resources not only as numbers to balance but as opportunities to further mission. Pastors show generosity when they offer their presence to those in need, even when their schedules are full. Chairs show generosity when they lead with patience, creating space for every voice to be heard. Officers and lay leaders show generosity when they give themselves to quiet acts of service that sustain the life of the church.

The promise of Proverbs is that generosity enriches not only those who receive but also those who give. Renewal flows from open hands. Leaders who live generously often discover that their own spirits are refreshed. The very act of giving—time, encouragement, wisdom, or resources—draws them closer to God's abundance.

Yet generosity requires trust. Leaders who already feel stretched thin may fear that giving more will lead to burnout. But the wisdom of scripture points to the opposite: those who give water will themselves be given water. Renewal comes not from hoarding time and energy but from sharing them in ways that align with God's purposes. This does not mean saying "yes" to every demand. It means discerning where generosity will bear fruit and trusting God to replenish what is poured out.

Communal stewardship grows from this same principle. A congregation led by fearful, withholding leaders often mirrors that scarcity. But when leaders model generosity—of time, talent, or assets—the whole community learns to live with open hands. Such a culture transforms how the church views its mission: not as survival but as participation in God's abundance.

The Ministry of Money reminds us that stewardship is deeply spiritual. It is not about clinging to control but about aligning resources with God's call. When leaders lead generously, they reframe the conversation. Instead of asking, "What do we lack?" they ask, "What can we give?" This shift creates renewal both for leaders and for the communities they guide.

Generosity also prevents burnout by re-centering leadership in joy. Leaders who give begrudgingly or under compulsion often become weary. But those who give freely, out of gratitude and trust, discover that generosity itself is life-giving. In serving others, they encounter the Spirit who refreshes.

As you reflect today, remember that your calling is not to preserve yourself by withholding but to trust God enough to give. Generosity does not leave you empty—it draws you into the abundance of God's kingdom, where giving and receiving are part of the same flow of grace.

Application

Reflect on one area of leadership where you are tempted to hold back—whether time, encouragement, or a specific talent. Write down one way you could practice generosity in that area this week. If you are with a group, share your reflections and ask: *How can our leadership embody generosity in a way that enriches both the giver and the community?*

_____

_____

_____

_____

_____

_____

_____

_____

_____

Prayer

Generous God, You refresh us even as You call us to refresh others. Teach us to lead with open hands, to share our time, talents, and resources with joy. Free us from the fear of scarcity, and help us trust Your promise that generosity brings renewal. Enrich us as we give, and may our leadership reflect Your abundance and sustain the life of Your church. Amen.

Day 27

"But don't begin until you count the cost. For who would begin construction of a building without first getting estimates and then checking to see if he has enough money to pay the bills?"

— Luke 14:28 (TLB)

Reflection

Jesus' words remind us that stewardship is not only about generosity—it is also about wisdom, planning, and accountability. Leaders are called to be visionaries, but also realists. Dreams without discipline lead to disappointment. Faithful stewardship requires counting the cost, discerning what resources are available, and making choices that align mission with capacity.

For treasurers, this principle is a daily reality. Balancing budgets, monitoring expenses, and planning for the future are not distractions from ministry; they are vital acts of stewardship. A congregation's financial integrity is part of its witness. Careful planning ensures that the church can meet commitments, support its mission, and respond to God's call without being crushed by debt or fear.

Pastors, too, live this wisdom when they pace themselves in ministry. Sermons, pastoral care, and visioning cannot be sustained without rest and boundaries. Counting the cost means recognizing human limits and leading with honesty about what is possible. Chairs of boards or councils count the cost when they prepare agendas thoughtfully, weigh options carefully, and guide conversations with clarity. Officers and lay leaders count the cost when they commit to roles of service with awareness of what those commitments require.

This verse also challenges leaders to resist impulsive or fear-driven decision-making. Counting the cost does not mean shrinking from bold action—it means ensuring that boldness is grounded in preparation. A church may feel called to expand its ministries, renovate facilities, or launch new outreach. These are good and faithful desires, but they must be accompanied by careful discernment. Planning is not a lack of faith; it is faith expressed in stewardship.

At the same time, counting the cost reminds us of the value of sacrifice. Jesus speaks these words in the context of discipleship, where the cost is not only financial but personal. Leadership requires giving of ourselves—our time, our energy, our talents—in ways that sometimes stretch us. Yet renewal comes when we count this cost in the light of Christ's call. Sacrifice without purpose leads to burnout. Sacrifice embraced as participation in God's mission leads to joy.

Communal stewardship grows from this shared practice of counting the cost together. Congregations that engage in open, honest conversations about resources cultivate trust. Leaders who bring transparency about finances, planning, and priorities invite the body to join in faithful discernment. In this way, counting the cost strengthens the whole community, preparing it not only to begin well but to finish faithfully.

Spirit-led stewardship holds planning and trust together. Leaders are called to prepare wisely, count resources carefully, and anticipate challenges honestly. At the same time, they are called to trust that God will provide what is needed for the mission. Renewal comes when leaders embrace both—planning diligently while remembering that the work is sustained by God's Spirit.

As you reflect on Jesus' words, consider what projects or responsibilities you face. Have you counted the cost? Are you stewarding resources wisely while also trusting God's provision? Faithful leadership balances vision with preparation, generosity with prudence, and mission with sustainability.

Application

Identify one responsibility or project in your leadership where you need to "count the cost." Write down the resources—time, talents, assets—needed to carry it out, and prayerfully consider whether they are aligned with your mission. If you are with a group, discuss together: *How can our leadership ensure that we begin only what we are prepared to sustain faithfully?*

Prayer

Wise and faithful God, You call us to dream boldly and to steward carefully. Teach us to count the cost of our commitments, to plan with integrity, and to trust Your provision. Free us from impulsive choices, and grant us the wisdom to align our time, talents, and resources with Your mission. Renew us as we lead, and help us to begin and finish with faithfulness. Amen.

Day 28

"I am the Lord All-Powerful, and I challenge you to put me to the test. Bring the entire ten percent into the storehouse, so there will be food in my house. Then I will open the windows of heaven and flood you with blessing after blessing."

— Malachi 3:10 (CEV)

Reflection

Malachi's bold challenge reminds us that stewardship is not merely a practical matter—it is a matter of trust. God speaks directly: bring the tithe, the whole of what is due, into the storehouse, and watch what I will do. For leaders, this is a profound reminder that generosity is not a transaction but an act of faith, one that opens the door to God's abundance.

Too often, stewardship in the church is framed primarily in terms of budgets and obligations. While accountability matters, Malachi's words lift stewardship into the realm of covenant. Giving of our time, talents, and assets is not only about sustaining the church—it is about entering into partnership with God's provision. God does not call us to give in order to diminish us, but to bless us and make blessing possible for others.

For treasurers, this passage reframes financial leadership. The tithe is not simply about revenue for programs; it is about ensuring that the "storehouse" of the church is full—so that ministry can flourish, so that no one is left hungry, so that God's mission is provided for. Pastors, in turn, can preach and teach stewardship not as duty but as discipleship, inviting people into the joy of trusting God with their best. Chairs and officers model this trust when they lead communities to prioritize generosity, even in seasons of scarcity, affirming that God's mission is not halted by fear.

The principle of the tithe also extends beyond money. Leaders are entrusted with time and talents that are meant to be offered generously. To give the "firstfruits" of our time means to place prayer, rest, and discernment before endless tasks. To give the best of our talents means offering them not for personal gain but for the good of the body. When leaders model this kind of giving, they remind their congregations that all we have belongs first to God.

Malachi's challenge is also an invitation to renewal. Burnout often comes when leaders view stewardship as extraction—always giving, always pouring out, without seeing fruit. But God promises that faithful stewardship opens the windows of heaven. Renewal comes when leaders shift from scarcity to abundance, trusting that their labor, their giving, and their faithfulness are met by God's overflowing grace. Leaders do not sustain the mission alone; they partner with a God who floods them with blessing.

This passage also teaches the communal power of stewardship. When leaders and congregations bring their full offering—time, talents, and resources—into the storehouse, the whole community is nourished. The church becomes a place of provision, generosity, and witness to the wider world. God's abundance is not for hoarding but for sharing, and leaders have the privilege of ensuring that the storehouse is open, full, and ready to bless.

Spirit-led stewardship requires courage. It asks leaders to trust that even when resources feel scarce, God's provision is enough. It challenges leaders to give faithfully, not grudgingly, and to invite others into that same joy. And it reminds leaders that the measure of stewardship is not simply in numbers but in the overflow of blessing that comes when God's people trust fully in God's care.

Application

Reflect on one area of your leadership—whether time, talent, or financial resource—where you are tempted to hold back out of fear. Write down one way you can practice fuller trust this week, offering your best to God. If you are with a group, discuss together: *What would it look like for us, as leaders, to bring our "firstfruits" into the storehouse of our shared ministry?*

_____

_____

_____

_____

_____

_____

_____

_____

Prayer

Abundant God, You promise to open the windows of heaven and pour out blessing when we trust You with our best. Teach us to give generously of our time, talents, and resources, not out of fear or duty but out of joy and gratitude. Renew us as we lead, and help us to create communities where Your abundance is shared freely, so that all may know Your sustaining love. Amen.

Day 29

"Now it is required that those who have been given a trust must prove faithful."

— 1 Corinthians 4:2 (NIV)

Reflection

Paul's words to the Corinthians go to the heart of stewardship: leadership is not ownership but trust. Everything leaders hold—time, talents, and assets—belongs first to God. The call is not to prove successful by human standards but to prove faithful in the trust we have been given.

Faithfulness, in this sense, means integrity, consistency, and alignment with God's purposes. For treasurers, it means handling financial resources with transparency and care, ensuring that every decision reflects the mission of the church. For pastors, it means offering gifts of preaching, teaching, and shepherding not for self-promotion but for the growth of the body. For chairs, it means guiding processes with fairness and prayer, building trust through how decisions are made as much as through what decisions are reached. For officers and lay leaders, it means showing up reliably, offering time and talents with humility, even when no one is watching.

Paul's reminder is sobering because faithfulness requires endurance. It is not a one-time act but a long-term posture. Leadership often involves seasons where results are unclear, where progress is slow, and where recognition is absent. Faithfulness presses forward anyway, trusting that God sees and honors what others may overlook. Leaders are not evaluated by immediate outcomes but by the steadiness of their trust in God's call.

This perspective brings renewal in seasons of discouragement. Burnout often comes when leaders measure themselves against unrealistic standards of success: growth in numbers, financial security, constant affirmation. Paul reframes the goal. Leadership is not about being spectacular; it is about being faithful. This truth frees leaders from the exhausting pursuit of perfection and invites them into the sustaining rhythm of consistency.

Communal renewal grows when congregations adopt this posture as well. Churches can become anxious when they measure success only by size, programs, or financial stability. But when leaders model faithfulness— steady trust, careful stewardship, consistent generosity—they shape a culture that values perseverance over performance. Such a culture is resilient, able to weather challenges without losing sight of its mission.

Spirit-led stewardship flows from this kind of faithfulness. Leaders who view their role as a sacred trust handle resources with reverence, recognizing that they are managing what belongs to God. They resist shortcuts, avoid manipulation, and act with integrity. They also model for the congregation that stewardship is not about control but about trust—living as though all that we have truly belongs to God.

Paul's call also reminds leaders that trust is relational. Leaders are entrusted by God but also by the community they serve. Congregations look to their leaders to be trustworthy stewards of time, talents, and assets. Faithfulness builds confidence within the body, allowing ministry to flourish in an atmosphere of trust.

As you reflect today, remember that faithfulness is less about extraordinary achievements and more about steady reliability. You may not always see the results of your leadership, but you can know that when you steward God's trust with integrity, you are fulfilling your calling.

Application

Identify one area of your leadership where you feel the pressure to prove successful. Reframe that area by asking: *What would faithfulness look like here, regardless of outcomes?* Write down one step you can take to act with integrity and trust this week. If you are with others, discuss: *How can we encourage one another to be faithful stewards of the trust given to us?*

_____

_____

_____

_____

_____

_____

_____

Prayer

Faithful God, You have entrusted us with time, talents, and resources for the sake of Your mission. Teach us to lead not for recognition but for faithfulness. Renew us when we are weary of chasing results, and anchor us in the assurance that You value our steady trust. May our leadership be marked by integrity, consistency, and devotion to Your purposes. Amen.

Day 30

"In everything I have shown you that, by working hard, we must help the weak. In this way we remember the Lord Jesus' words: 'It is more blessed to give than to receive.'"

— Acts 20:35 (CEB)

Reflection

Paul's farewell words to the Ephesian elders bring together stewardship, leadership, and mission in one powerful sentence. He does not simply instruct them to guard doctrine or organize structure; he calls them to remember the example of Jesus. To lead faithfully is to live generously, to use resources not for self-preservation but for service, especially to those most vulnerable.

Church leaders are entrusted with resources that carry spiritual weight. Treasurers manage finances, ensuring that the church can fulfill its commitments and invest in ministry. Pastors steward their time and presence, shaping the life of the congregation through teaching, care, and vision. Chairs steward the order and trust of governance, guiding decisions that affect how resources are used. Officers and lay leaders steward ministries that often operate quietly but sustain the whole body. Each of these roles is a trust, and each carries the same mandate: use resources to bless others, not to serve self-interest.

This call requires both generosity and diligence. Paul ties together "working hard" and "helping the weak." Stewardship is not passive—it is active, intentional, and often demanding. Leaders cannot shrug at their responsibilities, nor can they view them as purely transactional. Whether preparing budgets, allocating time, or managing people's gifts, leaders are called to labor faithfully, not for their own gain but for the sake of the community.

The words of Jesus—"It is more blessed to give than to receive"—anchor this teaching in the heart of discipleship. Giving is not a loss but a blessing. Leaders who live generously often find themselves renewed rather than depleted. The act of giving, when rooted in God's abundance, becomes life-giving both for those who receive and for those who lead. A treasurer who approaches financial stewardship as a ministry of generosity reframes the entire conversation. A pastor who offers time to those on the margins embodies Christ's blessing. A chair who ensures that governance decisions serve the mission rather than personal agendas practices this truth.

Yet stewardship is not only about the resources we hold—it is about the stories we tell with them. The way leaders use time, talents, and assets testifies to the congregation what it means to live faithfully. If leaders model fear, scarcity, or self-protection, the community learns to do the same. But if leaders embody generosity, transparency, and service, they invite the church into a culture of abundance and mission.

This teaching also provides protection against burnout. When leaders view stewardship as control—always striving to hold on tighter—they are quickly exhausted. But when leaders release resources into God's care, offering them generously, they find renewal. The work is not about hoarding or guarding but about giving and trusting. Leadership that embraces generosity as blessing is freed from the anxiety of scarcity and open to the joy of participation in God's abundance.

Paul's farewell reminds us that leadership itself is a resource. To lead is to give oneself in service. When leaders live this way, they mirror the generosity of Christ, who gave not only words but life. The blessing of leadership is not in recognition or reward but in the joy of giving—time, gifts, and presence—for the sake of the community and the mission of God.

Application

Identify one resource under your care—whether financial, personal time, or a particular talent—that you have been tempted to guard too closely. Write down one way you can use that resource more generously this week to bless others. If you are with a group, share your reflections and ask: *How can our leadership model generosity in a way that strengthens the mission of our church?*

_____

_____

_____

_____

_____

_____

Prayer

Generous Lord, You remind us that it is more blessed to give than to receive. Teach us to steward the resources entrusted to us with diligence and generosity. Free us from fear and scarcity, and help us to use our time, talents, and assets in ways that serve Your mission and bless others. Renew us as we give, and let our leadership reflect the generosity of Christ, who gave everything for the life of the world. Amen.

Day 31

"Then he was told, 'Go, stand on the mountain at attention before God. God will pass by.' A hurricane wind ripped through the mountains and shattered the rocks before God, but God wasn't to be found in the wind; after the wind an earthquake, but God wasn't in the earthquake; and after the earthquake fire, but God wasn't in the fire; and after the fire a gentle and quiet whisper."

— 1 Kings 19:11–12 (MSG)

Reflection

Elijah's encounter on the mountain is a profound lesson in discernment. He expected God to appear in the dramatic forces of wind, earthquake, and fire. Yet God chose to reveal Himself in a gentle and quiet whisper. For leaders, this story is both humbling and instructive. Discernment rarely comes in spectacle. More often, it comes in stillness.

Church leaders live in constant noise. Budgets, meetings, conflict, and competing demands can feel like hurricanes tearing through the mountains. Decisions press in like earthquakes shaking the ground beneath us. Urgent issues flare up like fire demanding immediate attention. It is easy to assume God's direction will be found in the most dramatic or pressing voice. But the story reminds us: God's whisper is often missed if we do not pause to listen.

Discernment begins with attention. Elijah is told to stand before God and wait. Leaders, too, must cultivate a posture of presence—creating space where God's quiet guidance can be heard. This is not passive inactivity but intentional openness. It may take the form of silent prayer before a difficult meeting, or pausing to breathe before responding in conflict. Discernment requires leaders to resist the pull of urgency long enough to make space for God's whisper.

This whisper does not negate the reality of storms, quakes, and fire. Leaders will face crises, conflicts, and urgency. But discernment reminds us that God's direction is not controlled by chaos. The Spirit speaks beyond the noise, guiding leaders to act with clarity rather than reaction. Renewal flows from this practice, for burnout often comes when leaders chase every fire. Discernment allows them to respond to God rather than to pressure.

Communal discernment mirrors this dynamic. Congregations can be swept up by urgent debates, loudest voices, or most dramatic needs. Yet when leaders model attentiveness to the Spirit's whisper, they help the community slow down and listen together. Discernment becomes less about winning arguments and more about hearing God's direction as one body.

The discernment spiral described in Sacred Listening echoes this rhythm: listening deeply, pausing for reflection, and circling back with greater clarity. Leadership discernment is not a one-time event but a process of returning again and again to the whisper of God. Each pause, each prayer, each moment of attention deepens the community's ability to hear and follow the Spirit.

Spirit-led stewardship of discernment requires humility. Leaders cannot control when or how God will speak. They can only create space, cultivate stillness, and remain open. This humility guards against burnout by reminding leaders that the future of the church does not rest solely on their shoulders. Discernment is shared. Direction comes from God, not from the noise or urgency of the moment.

As you reflect today, remember Elijah's lesson: the whisper carried more weight than the wind, the quake, or the fire. Discernment is not about force but about presence. Leaders who lean into that quiet voice find strength to guide their communities with peace, patience, and trust in God's gentle direction.

Application

Set aside ten minutes of silence today. No agenda, no requests—simply sit before God and listen. Write down any impressions, feelings, or whispers that emerge. If you are with others, practice a shared silence, and afterward ask together: *Where might God be speaking to us, not in noise or urgency, but in quiet trust?*

_____

_____

_____

_____

_____

_____

_____

Prayer

God of the whisper, teach us to listen beyond the noise. Calm the storms within and around us, and open our hearts to Your quiet guidance. Renew us with the assurance that You are present, not only in the dramatic moments but in the stillness that sustains us. Help us lead with patience, humility, and attentiveness, guiding Your people in step with Your Spirit. Amen.

Day 32

"If any of you is lacking in wisdom, ask God, who gives to all generously and ungrudgingly, and it will be given you."

— James 1:5 (NRSVue)

Reflection

James reminds us that discernment begins with humility. Leaders are not expected to have every answer, nor are they called to rely on their own cleverness. Instead, they are invited to ask—directly, honestly, and persistently—for wisdom. God, James assures us, delights in giving generously and without hesitation. This promise anchors leadership in dependence on God rather than on our own strength.

In leadership, wisdom is often more important than knowledge. Knowledge can tally budgets, organize agendas, and recall facts. Wisdom discerns when to pause, when to speak, and when to act. It sees beyond immediate circumstances into the deeper purposes of God. Leaders who seek wisdom acknowledge that governance, stewardship, and ministry cannot be sustained on information alone; they require the Spirit's guidance.

Discernment is not a one-time event but a continual spiral, as described in *Sacred Listening*. Leaders return again and again to God in prayer, listen deeply, reflect communally, and circle back with renewed clarity. Each turn of the spiral brings fresh insight. Each pause to ask for wisdom cultivates greater openness to God's voice. This rhythm prevents leadership from becoming reactive, grounded instead in a steady attentiveness to God's direction.

For treasurers, asking for wisdom may mean seeking clarity about how to interpret financial realities faithfully, balancing prudence with generosity. For pastors, it may mean discerning how to preach with truth and grace in challenging times. For chairs, it may mean guiding meetings in ways that honor both mission and people. For officers and lay leaders, it may mean knowing when to step forward in service and when to encourage others to lead. In every case, the promise holds: God will give wisdom, generously and ungrudgingly.

This truth is also communal. Leaders are called not only to ask for wisdom personally but to invite their communities into that same posture of prayerful dependence. Congregations often assume decisions must be made quickly or efficiently. But when leaders model discernment—slowing down, asking God for guidance, and waiting with trust—they teach the whole church that its direction comes not from human agendas but from God's generous wisdom.

Renewal flows from this posture. Burnout often comes when leaders feel the crushing expectation to have every solution ready. James offers freedom: you do not need to know everything, but you do need to ask. God's wisdom is not rationed, nor is it reserved for a select few. It is given to all who ask, because God desires to guide the church through Spirit-led leaders who are willing to listen.

The mission of the church depends on this kind of discernment. Without it, leaders risk confusing activity with purpose, urgency with calling, and human ambition with God's vision. But with it, the church can move faithfully, rooted in the assurance that its direction is grounded not in human wisdom but in divine generosity.

As you reflect on James' words, hear the invitation: ask boldly, ask continually, and ask together. Wisdom is not a scarce commodity. It is a gift, poured out abundantly for those willing to seek it.

Application

Set aside a decision you are currently facing in your leadership. Write it down, and then pray James 1:5 over it: *"God, I ask You for wisdom."* Sit in silence for a few minutes, trusting God's generous promise. If you are with a group, invite each person to name a decision they are carrying, pray together for wisdom, and listen for how God may be speaking.

_____

_____

_____

_____

_____

_____

_____

Prayer

Generous God, You promise to give wisdom freely to all who ask. We confess that we often try to lead in our own strength. Teach us to turn first to You, trusting that You delight to guide us. Renew us in patience and humility, and help us to model discernment that flows from Your Spirit. Grant us wisdom that sustains our leadership and aligns us with Your mission. Amen.

Day 33

"For the Lord grants wisdom! His every word is a treasure of knowledge and understanding. He grants good sense to the godly—his saints—he is their shield, protecting them and guarding their pathway."

— Proverbs 2:6–7 (TLB)

Reflection

Wisdom is not manufactured by human willpower or cleverness; it is granted by God. Proverbs reminds us that wisdom flows from the Lord, and every word of God is a treasure to those who seek it. For leaders, this truth is essential. Discernment is not about mastering techniques or relying on our instincts alone—it is about turning toward God as the source of all understanding.

Leadership in the church often demands decisions that do not have clear or simple answers. How should resources be allocated? Which ministries should be prioritized? How do we navigate conflict faithfully? These moments require more than quick judgment; they require discernment rooted in God's wisdom. When leaders turn to God in prayer, listen to Scripture, and invite the Spirit's guidance, they tap into a treasure far greater than their own abilities.

The language of Proverbs also assures leaders of God's protection. Wisdom is not only a gift of knowledge but a shield for the faithful. Leaders who ground their decisions in God's wisdom are guarded against rashness, self-interest, or fear. They are equipped to walk securely, even when the path is uncertain. This does not mean challenges will disappear, but it does mean leaders can trust God's guidance to carry them through.

Discernment, as described in *Sacred Listening*, is a spiral rather than a straight line. It calls leaders to return again and again to God—listening deeply, reflecting carefully, and circling back with new clarity. Each cycle brings leaders closer to alignment with God's will. This practice slows the frantic pace of leadership, inviting renewal through attentiveness. Burnout often comes when leaders believe they must rely solely on their own sense of direction. Renewal comes when they recognize that God's wisdom is a shield, protecting them as they listen and wait.

Communal discernment builds on this same rhythm. A congregation that seeks wisdom together—through prayer, dialogue, and listening—creates a culture of trust. Instead of rushing to majority votes or defaulting to the loudest voices, communities that pause to seek God's word find that decisions become more faithful and less divisive. Leaders who model this posture remind the church that discernment is not just about efficiency but about alignment with God's mission.

This wisdom also speaks directly to stewardship. Leaders are entrusted not only with finances and resources but with the very life of the church. Stewardship guided by human anxiety can lead to either reckless risk or fearful stagnation. Stewardship guided by God's wisdom invites balance, creativity, and courage. Leaders who seek divine wisdom learn to steward resources in ways that honor God's abundance rather than human scarcity.

As you reflect today, remember that discernment is not about perfection or always knowing the right answer in advance. It is about trust—believing that God delights in granting wisdom, that God's word is a treasure, and that God's wisdom provides protection for those who seek it. Leaders are called to be seekers first, trusting that the One who grants wisdom will guide the way.

Application

Think of a decision in your leadership where you feel uncertain. Pause today to read Proverbs 2:6–7 slowly, inviting God's wisdom into your discernment. Write down one word or phrase that stands out to you, and reflect on how it might guide your next step. If you are with others, read the passage aloud together and ask: *What wisdom is God granting us for this moment?*

_____

_____

_____

_____

_____

_____

_____

_____

Prayer

God of wisdom, You are the source of knowledge, understanding, and protection. Teach us to seek Your voice above our own instincts, and remind us that every word You speak is a treasure. Guard our steps as we lead, and grant us the good sense to walk in Your ways. Renew our courage to listen deeply, discern faithfully, and serve with trust in Your wisdom. Amen.

Day 34

"The Spirit shows what is true and will come and guide you into the full truth. The Spirit doesn't speak on its own. It will tell you only what it has heard from me, and it will let you know what is going to happen."

— John 16:13 (CEV)

Reflection

Jesus' promise to his disciples is a profound assurance for leaders who face the weight of discernment. He does not leave his followers to navigate on their own. Instead, he promises the Spirit, who will guide them into all truth. Leadership in the church is not sustained by human wisdom alone but by the Spirit who continues to speak, lead, and reveal what is true.

Discernment often feels overwhelming. Leaders must make decisions with limited information, balancing competing needs and pressures. Yet Jesus reminds us that discernment is not a solitary exercise—it is a Spirit-led journey. The Spirit guides not in sudden flashes of certainty alone but through an ongoing process of listening, reflecting, and responding. This is the rhythm described in *Sacred Listening*: pausing to hear, circling back with openness, and moving forward in faith.

The Spirit's role is both revelatory and reassuring. Leaders may not know the full picture, but they can trust that the Spirit speaks what is needed for the next step. The Spirit does not create new truth apart from Christ but faithfully communicates what has been heard from him. This grounds discernment not in speculation but in the living voice of God. For leaders, this means that decisions—whether about finances, mission priorities, or pastoral care—can be approached with confidence that God is actively guiding.

For treasurers, discernment may involve listening for how resources can be aligned with mission rather than mere preservation. For pastors, it may mean hearing how to speak truth into moments of uncertainty. For chairs, it may mean discerning how to hold space for both vision and unity in leadership gatherings. For officers and lay leaders, it may mean recognizing when their quiet service is precisely the Spirit's way of sustaining the body. In each case, the Spirit's whisper continues to guide.

Communal discernment is also central here. Jesus speaks to his disciples as a group, not only as individuals. The Spirit's guidance is often clearest when the community listens together, testing insights against Scripture, prayer, and shared reflection. This is why discernment in the church is never simply private intuition but a shared search for truth. Leaders who cultivate this practice invite their communities into deeper trust—not in their own authority but in the Spirit's presence among them.

This posture also guards against burnout. Leaders who assume they must carry the weight of perfect decision-making often collapse under the pressure. But when leaders remember that discernment belongs to the Spirit, not to them alone, they can rest. Renewal comes when leaders shift from striving to listening, from anxiety to trust. The Spirit is still speaking, and leaders are simply called to pay attention.

Ultimately, discernment is not about predicting the future but about trusting the Spirit to reveal the way forward step by step. Leaders who rely on the Spirit model for their congregations a way of life rooted in dependence and hope. They show that the truth is not manufactured by human effort but revealed by the God who delights in guiding his people.

Application

Choose one decision facing your leadership right now. Spend time in prayer, asking specifically for the Spirit's guidance. Then listen in silence for several minutes. Write down any impressions or words that come to mind. If you are with others, invite the group to practice this same silence together, and afterward ask: *What might the Spirit be guiding us toward as we seek the truth?*

_____

_____

_____

_____

_____

_____

_____

_____

Prayer

Spirit of Truth, You continue to guide us as Jesus promised. Teach us to listen with open hearts and to trust that You speak what we most need to hear. Free us from the illusion that we lead alone, and remind us that discernment is Your gift. Renew our strength as we listen, and guide us into the truth that aligns our leadership with Christ's mission. Amen.

Day 35

"He says, 'Be still, and know that I am God; I will be exalted among the nations, I will be exalted in the earth.'"

— Psalm 46:10 (NIV)

Reflection

Discernment begins with stillness. In a world of constant noise and endless demands, God's invitation to "be still" is both countercultural and life-giving. Leaders in the church often feel pressured to act quickly, to respond immediately, to solve every problem at once. Yet the psalmist reminds us that clarity comes not from striving but from pausing, remembering who God is, and resting in the assurance of God's sovereignty.

Stillness is not inactivity. It is attentiveness. It is the practice of creating space where God's voice can be heard above the noise. In *Sacred Listening*, this is described as part of the discernment spiral: stepping back, listening deeply, reflecting, and then moving forward with renewed clarity. For leaders, this practice is not a luxury but a necessity. Without it, decisions are made in haste, and leadership becomes reactionary rather than Spirit-led.

For treasurers, stillness might mean pausing before the numbers, remembering that budgets are not only financial tools but reflections of faith and mission. For pastors, it might mean stepping away from the pressure of constant production to listen for God's word before speaking to God's people. For chairs, it might mean guiding meetings with moments of silence, trusting that discernment is not only found in discussion but also in listening together. For officers and lay leaders, it might mean slowing down enough to recognize the Spirit's nudge in their acts of service.

The psalmist ties stillness to the knowledge of God: "Be still, and know that I am God." Discernment is grounded not in human ability but in divine presence. Leaders do not need to carry the burden of knowing everything or predicting outcomes. They are invited to trust that God is at work, even when the path is not yet clear. This awareness renews leaders, reminding them that their role is not to manufacture certainty but to listen faithfully.

Communal discernment also depends on stillness. Congregations that rush into decisions without pausing to pray and reflect risk mistaking urgency for clarity. But when communities embrace stillness—whether through shared silence, intentional prayer, or slowing the pace of decision-making—they open themselves to God's guidance. Leaders who model this practice teach their congregations that discernment is not about efficiency but about attentiveness to God.

Stillness also guards against burnout. Leaders who never pause are consumed by the urgency of every demand. Renewal comes when they release control, even for a moment, and remember that God is exalted in the earth regardless of their striving. To be still is to remember that the church belongs to God first, and its future is sustained by God's faithfulness.

As you reflect today, hear the psalm not as a suggestion but as a command: *be still.* Discernment begins here—with the courage to stop, listen, and trust that God is present, speaking, and guiding the way forward.

Application

Take five minutes today to sit in complete silence, repeating the words of Psalm 46:10: *"Be still, and know that I am God."* Notice how your thoughts and feelings shift as you rest in God's presence. If you are with others, begin a meeting with shared silence, and afterward reflect together: *What did we hear in the stillness that might guide our next steps?*

_____

_____

_____

_____

_____

_____

_____

_____

_____

Prayer

God of stillness and strength, teach us to pause in the midst of our busyness and remember that You are God. Quiet the noise around us and within us, so that we may hear Your voice. Renew our trust in Your presence, and guide our leadership with patience and peace. Help us to model stillness for our communities, that we may discern faithfully and follow where You lead. Amen.

Day 36

"The Holy Spirit has led us to the decision that no burden should be placed on you other than these essentials."

— Acts 15:28 (CEB)

Reflection

The early church faced a moment of profound discernment at the council in Jerusalem. Tensions were high as leaders debated whether new believers should be bound by longstanding traditions and practices. The stakes were not only theological but deeply practical—what kind of community would the church become? In the midst of debate, the apostles and elders reached a conclusion that carried both authority and humility: *"The Holy Spirit has led us to the decision."*

This verse underscores the heart of discernment. Decisions in the church are not simply matters of majority vote or compromise. They are the result of listening to the Spirit and seeking unity in mission. The leaders did not claim personal authority but acknowledged that their conclusion arose from the Spirit's guidance. For leaders today, this reminder is essential: discernment is less about enforcing our own opinions and more about aligning with the Spirit's direction.

The process described here echoes what *Sacred Listening* calls the discernment spiral: listening deeply, reflecting communally, returning again to prayer, and moving forward with clarity. The council in Acts 15 did not arrive quickly at consensus. They wrestled, listened, and tested their conclusions against the mission of Christ. This patient, prayerful process is what allowed them to say with confidence that the Spirit had led them.

For treasurers, this kind of discernment may mean prayerfully considering how financial decisions affect not only the bottom line but the mission of the church. For pastors, it may mean listening deeply to both Scripture and the lived experience of the community before offering guidance. For chairs, it may mean guiding difficult conversations in ways that create space for prayer and attentiveness rather than rushing to a decision. For officers and lay leaders, it may mean trusting that even in the details of service, the Spirit's guidance shapes the larger picture of the church's life.

The council's conclusion is striking not only for its reliance on the Spirit but also for its restraint: *"no burden should be placed on you other than these essentials."* Discernment often requires leaders to distinguish between what is essential and what is unnecessary. Burnout frequently arises when leaders place too many burdens on themselves or their communities—extra expectations, traditions, or anxieties that obscure the heart of the mission. Renewal comes when leaders remember that the Spirit often calls us to simplicity: focusing on essentials that sustain the community's life and witness.

Communal renewal flows from this posture. When leaders seek discernment together with humility, acknowledging the Spirit's presence, congregations experience trust and clarity. The work of leadership becomes less about control and more about listening. The Spirit's guidance frees communities from unnecessary burdens and directs their energy toward what truly matters: loving God and serving others.

As you reflect on this passage, remember that discernment is not about having all the answers. It is about trusting the Spirit's presence in the midst of debate, listening patiently for clarity, and choosing simplicity over unnecessary complexity. Leaders who cultivate this posture will not only avoid burnout but also guide their communities into deeper trust in God's leading.

Application

Think of a decision your leadership group is currently facing. Ask together: *What feels essential for faithfulness, and what might be an unnecessary burden?* Spend time in prayer before discussing, inviting the Spirit to guide you toward clarity. Write down one step you can take to simplify the decision and align it more closely with God's mission.

_____

_____

_____

_____

_____

_____

_____

Prayer

Spirit of Truth, we thank You for guiding the church in every age. Teach us to listen as the apostles did, to seek unity, and to discern what is truly essential. Free us from placing unnecessary burdens on ourselves or others, and lead us into the simplicity of Your mission. Renew our courage to trust that You are with us in every decision, guiding us into life and freedom. Amen.

Day 37

"Put God in charge of your work, then what you've planned will take place."

— Proverbs 16:3 (MSG)

Reflection

Discernment is often caught between two tensions: the desire to plan carefully and the call to trust deeply. Leaders know the importance of preparation—budgets must balance, ministries must be organized, and responsibilities must be met. Yet Proverbs reminds us that plans alone are not enough. When leaders surrender their work to God, aligning their vision with God's purposes, their plans are given life and direction.

This surrender is not passive. It does not mean abandoning planning or careful leadership. Rather, it means placing God at the center of every decision, allowing divine wisdom to shape the course. Discernment is not the absence of planning but the offering of plans to God for refinement, redirection, or confirmation.

For treasurers, this might mean preparing a budget not as a spreadsheet alone but as a prayerful act, asking how resources can best serve God's mission. For pastors, it might mean crafting sermons and strategies with openness to how the Spirit might change direction midstream. For chairs, it might mean preparing agendas but holding space for holy interruptions. For officers and lay leaders, it might mean offering their service not simply as tasks but as part of God's larger work.

Sacred Listening's spiral reflects this dynamic well: listen, reflect, test, and return again. Leaders bring their plans to God in prayer, listen for the Spirit's whisper, reflect communally, and discern whether the work aligns with God's mission. Over time, this rhythm shapes leaders into people who both prepare faithfully and trust deeply.

Placing God in charge of our work is also an act of freedom. Many leaders are weighed down by the pressure of outcomes. Success is measured by attendance, giving, or visible results. Yet Proverbs reminds us that the work does not ultimately rest on human effort. When God is in charge, leaders are freed from anxiety about outcomes and renewed in their trust that God's purposes will be fulfilled. This posture prevents burnout, as leaders release the illusion that everything depends on them.

Communal discernment grows when leaders model this surrender. Congregations learn from their leaders how to hold plans lightly, to prepare faithfully, and to release outcomes into God's hands. Such communities embody a balance of diligence and trust, planning carefully while remaining open to the Spirit's movement.

Discernment requires humility. It means admitting that even our best-laid plans may not align with God's purposes. It also requires courage—the courage to act when the Spirit confirms, and the courage to change direction when God calls for something new. Renewal flows from this posture, as leaders discover the joy of being co-laborers with God rather than sole architects of the future.

As you reflect today, consider how your leadership might shift if God were placed fully in charge of your work. Discernment begins here: with planning shaped not by fear or control, but by trust that God delights to direct the steps of those who listen.

Application

Take one plan you are currently developing in your leadership. Pray Proverbs 16:3 over it: *"Put God in charge of your work, then what you've planned will take place."* Ask God to refine, redirect, or affirm your plan. If you are with a group, invite each person to share one plan they are holding and pray together, offering each plan to God's guidance.

_____

_____

_____

_____

_____

_____

_____

Prayer

God of wisdom and direction, we offer You the work entrusted to us. Teach us to prepare with diligence but to trust with openness. Free us from the burden of outcomes, and align our plans with Your mission. Renew us with courage to act where You confirm and humility to change where You redirect. May all that we do bear witness to Your presence guiding our steps. Amen.

Day 38

"Then the Lord answered me and said: Write the vision; make it plain on tablets, so that a runner may read it. For there is still a vision for the appointed time; it speaks of the end and does not lie. If it seems to tarry, wait for it; it will surely come, it will not delay."

— Habakkuk 2:2–3 (NRSVue)

Reflection

Discernment is not only about listening for God's direction in the present moment but also about carrying vision into the future with patience and clarity. The prophet Habakkuk is instructed to write the vision and make it plain, ensuring that it could be read even in motion, by someone running. The promise is that God's vision will come at its appointed time—though it may feel slow, it will not fail.

For leaders, this passage is both encouragement and challenge. It affirms that God gives vision, not as vague possibilities but as clear direction. Leaders are called to listen deeply for God's voice and then articulate what they hear in ways the community can understand. Discernment that remains private or unclear does little to guide the body. Writing the vision and making it plain means speaking in language that is accessible, practical, and grounded in the mission of God.

At the same time, Habakkuk reminds us that vision unfolds on God's timeline, not ours. Leaders often feel pressure to produce results quickly, to show evidence that the vision is working. But discernment requires patience. The Spirit's direction may take time to become visible, and rushing ahead can create confusion or burnout. Faithful leaders trust that God's promises are sure, even when the waiting feels long.

This teaching resonates with *Sacred Listening*'s discernment spiral. Leaders listen for God's voice, reflect on what they hear, articulate the vision, and then return to listening again. Each cycle may bring greater clarity, refining the vision until it can be made plain for others. In this process, patience is essential. Vision discerned too quickly may lack depth; vision discerned patiently is grounded in God's timing.

For treasurers, this passage might mean articulating financial clarity that supports mission, making numbers "plain" so all can see the story they tell. For pastors, it might mean preaching or teaching vision in ways that both inspire and guide. For chairs, it may mean writing agendas or leading conversations that keep the mission clear and central. For officers and lay leaders, it may mean embodying the vision in small, steady acts of service that make the larger mission visible.

Communal discernment depends on clarity. Congregations often falter when vision is muddled or when leaders assume people will simply "catch on." Habakkuk's instruction reminds us that vision must be communicated plainly and consistently. Renewal comes when leaders make God's direction visible, allowing the whole community to run together toward God's future.

Burnout is eased when leaders release the pressure to make the vision happen by sheer force. Discernment invites leaders to trust that the vision is God's, not theirs. Their task is to listen, to write it plainly, and to wait faithfully. Renewal flows from this trust, as leaders are freed from frantic striving and anchored in hope.

As you reflect on Habakkuk's words, consider how vision is communicated in your leadership. Is it plain enough for all to see? Are you willing to wait for its fulfillment in God's time? Discernment is both clarity and patience—writing what God reveals and trusting that it will surely come.

Application

Take a vision currently guiding your leadership—whether for a ministry, budget, or community initiative—and write it out in one or two sentences. Make it plain enough that anyone could understand its purpose. If you are with others, share these sentences and ask: *Does this vision reflect God's mission for us, and is it clear enough for us to carry together?*

_____

_____

_____

_____

_____

_____

_____

Prayer

God of vision and promise, You speak into our waiting hearts and guide us toward Your future. Teach us to listen deeply, to write plainly, and to trust patiently. Free us from the urgency of our own timelines, and anchor us in the assurance that Your vision will surely come. Renew our courage to lead with clarity, humility, and hope, so that our communities may run together in step with Your Spirit. Amen.

Day 39

"If you leave God's paths and go astray, you will hear a Voice behind you say, 'No, this is the way; walk here.'"

— Isaiah 30:21 (TLB)

Reflection

Isaiah's promise offers profound reassurance to leaders: even when we stray, God does not abandon us. Instead, God's voice follows us, calling us back to the path we are meant to walk. Discernment is not about flawless decision-making but about cultivating attentiveness to this guiding voice. The heart of leadership is not perfection but faithfulness—listening, returning, and realigning with God's way.

Leaders often face choices that are not clear-cut. Should resources be used for one ministry or another? Should the church move forward with bold change or remain steady? Should leaders speak out or remain silent? In these moments, the temptation is either to freeze in indecision or to move ahead in self-reliance. Isaiah reminds us that God's guidance is not distant but near. The Spirit speaks, often gently, to redirect us when we wander.

This aligns with *Sacred Listening*'s discernment spiral. Discernment is not a straight line from question to answer; it is a process of listening, pausing, reflecting, and adjusting. Leaders may not always choose perfectly, but they can trust that God will keep calling them back. Each cycle of listening and returning draws them closer to alignment with God's mission.

For treasurers, this voice may be heard in the tug to prioritize faithfulness over fear when interpreting financial realities. For pastors, it may come as a whisper to preach a hard but needed word. For chairs, it may guide them to slow a meeting when decisions are being rushed. For officers and lay leaders, it may speak in the quiet assurance that their unseen service matters profoundly to the life of the church. In every role, discernment is less about mastering control and more about staying attuned to the Spirit's direction.

This passage also carries a message of grace. Leaders can easily feel crushed by mistakes, fearing that one wrong step could derail a congregation. But Isaiah reminds us that God's guidance continues even after missteps. The voice behind us does not scold or condemn but gently redirects: "No, this is the way." This assurance brings renewal. Leaders do not have to bear the burden of flawless leadership; they are called instead to responsive leadership—listening, adjusting, and trusting God's faithful guidance.

Communal discernment depends on this same posture. Congregations may wander into fear, distraction, or division, but God's voice continues to call them back to the way of faithfulness. Leaders who model attentive listening help their communities to hear and trust that voice together. Discernment, then, becomes less about control and more about mutual attentiveness to the Spirit's redirection.

Burnout often comes when leaders believe they must get everything right the first time. Renewal comes when they remember that discernment is a journey, not a test. God's voice continues to accompany us, offering course corrections and guidance along the way. The gift of discernment is not certainty but presence—the assurance that God walks with us, guiding us step by step.

As you reflect today, hear Isaiah's promise as both comfort and challenge. God's voice is speaking. The question is: are you listening closely enough to hear the whisper that says, "This is the way; walk here"?

Application

Take time today to reflect on a recent decision where you may have felt uncertain or even mistaken. Sit in silence, asking God to speak into that moment with clarity. Write down what you sense the Spirit whispering now. If you are with others, share your reflections and ask: *Where have we heard God's voice redirecting us as a community?*

_____

_____

_____

_____

_____

_____

_____

Prayer

Guiding God, we thank You for never leaving us to wander alone. When we stray, You speak with gentle clarity: "This is the way." Teach us to listen for Your voice in the noise of leadership and to trust Your presence in both our steps and missteps. Renew our courage to follow Your guidance, and help us lead our communities with humility, patience, and hope. Amen.

Day 40

"Put everything to the test. Accept what is good."

— 1 Thessalonians 5:21 (CEV)

Reflection

Paul's instruction to the Thessalonians offers a clear, practical framework for discernment: test everything, hold fast to what is good. For leaders in the church, this is both a caution and a promise. Discernment does not mean blindly accepting every idea, nor does it mean dismissing what is unfamiliar. It means prayerfully and communally testing, weighing, and discerning what aligns with God's mission.

In leadership, countless opportunities and challenges arise—new programs, financial decisions, governance structures, or pastoral initiatives. The temptation is either to rush forward without reflection or to resist every change out of fear. Paul calls leaders to a different path: test carefully, discern faithfully, and embrace what reflects the goodness of God.

This practice mirrors the discernment spiral described in *Sacred Listening*. Leaders are invited to listen deeply, reflect communally, test ideas against Scripture and prayer, and then return to listening again. Discernment is not static but iterative. By testing and re-testing, leaders gradually clarify what is life-giving for their community and what distracts from God's mission.

For treasurers, this may mean testing financial decisions not only by their practicality but by their faithfulness to the church's calling. For pastors, it may mean weighing words in a sermon or vision against the truth of the gospel and the needs of the people. For chairs, it may mean facilitating processes that allow ideas to be examined prayerfully rather than adopted hastily. For officers and lay leaders, it may mean discerning how their service contributes to the larger mission, ensuring that their efforts are aligned with God's purposes.

This passage also teaches leaders to value openness alongside caution. Testing is not the same as rejecting. It is a willingness to engage new ideas, perspectives, and practices with discernment. Leaders who embrace this balance model for their congregations a culture that is both rooted and responsive: grounded in faith, yet open to the Spirit's fresh movement.

Communal discernment is especially important here. Paul does not envision testing as a solitary act but as a shared process within the body of Christ. Leaders who invite their communities into testing ideas together—through prayer, dialogue, and reflection—strengthen trust and unity. This kind of shared discernment prevents burnout by reminding leaders that they are not called to carry the weight of decision-making alone.

Burnout often arises when leaders feel pressured to know everything or decide everything perfectly. Paul's words relieve that pressure: test everything, hold fast to the good. Leaders are not asked to solve every problem instantly or flawlessly. They are asked to engage faithfully, to seek God's guidance, and to cling to what aligns with the Spirit's work. Renewal flows from this rhythm, as leaders discover that discernment is a shared journey, not an individual burden.

As you reflect today, remember that discernment requires both courage and humility. Courage to test and explore, humility to let go of what does not serve God's mission. Leaders who embody this balance help their communities live into Paul's vision: a people who test everything faithfully and hold fast to what is good.

Application

Choose one decision or idea currently before you. Write down what excites you about it and what concerns you. Then ask: *How does this align with God's mission for our church?* If you are with a group, practice testing the idea together through prayer and conversation, asking the Spirit to reveal what is good and worth holding onto.

_____

_____

_____

_____

_____

_____

_____

Prayer

God of wisdom and truth, teach us to test all things with patience and faith. Free us from fear that rejects too quickly and from haste that accepts without reflection. Help us to discern what is good, to release what distracts, and to cling to what aligns with Your mission. Renew us as we lead, and guide our communities into deeper trust in Your Spirit's direction. Amen.

Final Word

You have walked through forty days of Scripture, reflection, prayer, and practice. These pages have not been the destination, but a path toward a deeper way of leading — one rooted in God's call, sustained by God's strength, aligned with God's resources, and attuned to the Spirit's whisper.

The journey of leadership does not end here. It continues each time you pause to pray before a decision, listen before you speak, or ask the Spirit to guide your steps. It deepens whenever you help your community remember its calling, whenever you release anxiety into God's hands, and whenever you steward faithfully the gifts entrusted to your care.

The Spirit who has led you through these days will keep leading you. The same God who called you will continue to renew you. The church you serve belongs first to Christ, who is faithful in every season.

Go forward, then, not in your own strength, but in the strength that comes from the One who called you. Lead with humility. Serve with joy. Listen for the quiet voice that says, "This is the way; walk in it." And may your leadership always point to the love of God made known in Jesus Christ.

Effective Church Leadership Community

Equipping Leaders to Serve Faithfully, Lead Boldly, and Follow the Spirit Together

Leadership in the church is sacred, courageous work. You don't have to do it alone.

The Effective Church Leadership Community is a free online space for pastors, treasurers, board members, and ministry leaders to connect, grow, and lead with clarity. Through webinars, tools, best practices, and supportive conversation, we help churches align energy and resources with God's calling — not alone, but together.

Whether you're stepping into leadership or guiding others, this community offers practical wisdom and spiritual encouragement for the road ahead.

Scan to join or visit the link below:

https://community.churchtrainingcenter.com

Continue the Journey

Your work as chairperson is part of a larger stream of Spirit-led leadership. Just as roots are nourished by surrounding soil, your leadership is enriched when supported by companions along the way. The following resources complement *Rooted in the Call*, providing depth, tools, and practices that sustain your service. Together they form a library of wisdom, each one strengthening your ability to guide the board with clarity, discernment, and hope. For further resources and templates, the Effective Church Leadership Community (ECLC) offers expanded support.

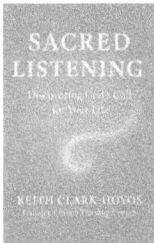

Sacred Listening: Discovering God's Call for Your Life
This devotional guide invites you into practices of silence, prayer, and discernment. It equips you to cultivate listening in your own life and to foster a board culture that waits upon the Spirit before acting.

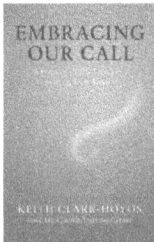

Embracing Our Call: A Practical Guide for Church Governing Body Leaders
This is the foundational textbook for Spirit-led governance. It helps you anchor your leadership in the Calling–Energy–Resources–Discernment framework, ensuring that the entire board aligns structure and mission.

Called Together: A Spirit-Led Discernment Guide for Congregational Planning
This guide offers nine phases of planning grounded in prayer and discernment. It supports your leadership by giving the congregation a shared process for shaping vision and mission faithfully.

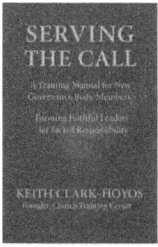

Serving the Call: A Training Manual for New Governance Body Members

This workbook provides practical exercises, templates, and examples to orient new board members. It strengthens your chairing by offering tools to train and equip others for Spirit-led governance.

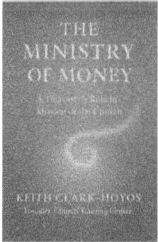

The Ministry of Money: A Treasurer's Role in the Mission of the Church

This book reframes the treasurer's work as a sacred ministry. It complements your leadership by ensuring that stewardship of money remains aligned with calling and mission, freeing you to guide with confidence.

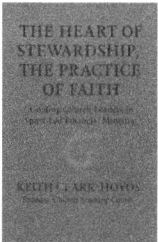

The Heart of Stewardship: The Practice of Faith

This workbook companion to *The Ministry of Money* offers practical tools for treasurers and finance committees. It reinforces your leadership by ensuring that financial stewardship is practiced with integrity and faith, bridging policy and mission.

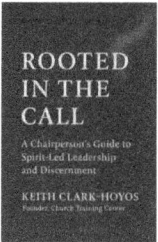

Rooted in the Call: A Chairperson's Guide to Spirit-Led Leadership and Discernment

This guide equips church chairpersons to see their role not as merely managing meetings but as stewarding mission. With reflections, practices, and tools, it helps leaders keep their governing body grounded in calling, aligned in discernment, and steady through seasons of change. It affirms the chairperson's sacred role as Mission Keeper, ensuring that all leadership flows from the Spirit's direction.

About the Author

Keith Clark-Hoyos is a dedicated leader known for his unwavering positivity and remarkable ability to guide and inspire within the realm of church leadership and administration. His life journey has been characterized by a deep commitment to personal and professional growth, a passion for teaching and coaching, and a profound love for nurturing individuals and organizations toward their highest potential.

In 2015, Keith transitioned from his role as a church judicatory leader to found Church Training Center — a thriving consulting, coaching, training, and accounting firm serving churches and nonprofits across the nation. Together with his wife and partner, he has built a team that supports mission-driven ministries with clarity, care, and Spirit-led wisdom.

Keith holds a Master of Arts in Ministry, Leadership & Service from Claremont School of Theology and an undergraduate degree in Business Administration and Church Ministries from Simpson University. He is also a Daoist Monk in the Wù Zhēn Pài (Awakened Reality Sect) lineage and brings a deeply contemplative and spiritually grounded presence to his work.

At the heart of Keith's calling is a desire to empower church leaders to live faithfully, lead effectively, and align all resources — financial, human, and spiritual — with the mission God has placed before them.

Scripture Index

Scripture Reference	Translation	Day
Romans 12:1	NRSVue	7
1 Corinthians 4:2	NIV	29
1 Corinthians 12:18	NIV	3
2 Corinthians 4:7–9	CEB	18
2 Corinthians 9:6–8	CEV	22
Galatians 6:9	NRSVue	14
Ephesians 4:1	MSG	5
Philippians 4:13	CEV	16
Colossians 1:11–12	TLB	15
1 Thessalonians 5:21	CEV	40
1 Timothy 6:17–19	MSG	25
James 1:5	NRSVue	32
Proverbs 2:6–7	TLB	33
Proverbs 3:9–10	NIV	23
Proverbs 11:25	NRSVue	26
Proverbs 16:3	MSG	37
Hebrews 12:1–2	NRSVue	20
1 Peter 4:10	NIV	8
1 Kings 19:11–12	MSG	31

www.ingramcontent.com/pod-product-compliance
Lightning Source LLC
Chambersburg PA
CBHW030830090426
42737CB00009B/955